ARTHUR JAMES BALFOUR, 1848–1930

Historiography and Annotated Bibliography

ARTHUR JAMES BALFOUR, 1848–1930

Historiography and Annotated Bibliography

Eugene L. Rasor

BIBLIOGRAPHIES OF
BRITISH STATESMEN, NO. 22

MYRON J. SMITH, JR., SERIES ADVISER

Greenwood Press

Westport, Connecticut • London

Library of Congress Cataloging-in-Publication Data

Rasor, Eugene L., 1936–
    Arthur James Balfour, 1848–1930 : historiography and annotated
bibliography / Eugene L. Rasor.
        p.   cm.—(Bibliographies of British statesmen, ISSN
1056–5515 ; no. 22)
    Includes indexes.
    ISBN 0–313–28877–1 (alk. paper)
    1. Balfour, Arthur James Balfour, Earl of, 1848–1930—
Bibliography.   2. Great Britain—Politics and
government—1837–1901—Bibliography.   3. Great Britain—Politics and
government—1901–1936—Bibliography.   4. Prime ministers—Great
Britain—Biography—Bibliography.   I. Title.   II. Series.
Z8068.78.R37   1998
[DA566.9.B2]
016.941082′092—dc21   98–27676

British Library Cataloguing in Publication Data is available.

Library of Congress Catalog Card Number: 98–27676
ISBN: 0–313–28877–1
ISSN: 1056–5515

First published in 1998

Greenwood Press, 88 Post Road West, Westport, CT 06881
An imprint of Greenwood Publishing Group, Inc.

Printed in the United States of America

The paper used in this book complies with the
Permanent Paper Standard issued by the National
Information Standards Organization (Z39.48–1984).

10 9 8 7 6 5 4 3 2 1

To Neel and Iris Rich

Contents

Acknowledgments

For some, the name of Arthur James Balfour is a household word. He was a British Prime Minister and signer of the famous Balfour Declaration calling for a national home for the Jews in Palestine. Less well known are his initiatives in creating a structure for strategic planning, preparation for, and fighting a war, the Committee of Imperial Defence, and chairing the committee which articulated the basis for the constitution of the British Commonwealth of Nations, the Balfour Report or Balfour Definition. And there is more, to be presented in the following chapters.

This is the ninth in a series of historiographical surveys-annotated bibliographies contracted by the author with Greenwood Press in its Bibliographies of Battles and Leaders and Bibliographies of British Statesmen series. The subjects of three have been famous leaders: General Douglas MacArthur, 1994, Earl Mountbatten of Burma, 1998, and this one, Arthur James Balfour. The others related to British naval history: The Spanish Armada, 1993, The Battle of Jutland, 1991, and The Falklands/Malvinas Campaign, 1991, or Campaigns of the Pacific War: The Solomon Islands Campaign, 1997, The Southwest Pacific Campaign, 1996, and The China-Burma-India Campaign, 1998. Contracts have been signed with Greenwood Press for two more: Winston S. Churchill in the Bibliographies of World Leaders series and English/British Naval History to 1815 in the Bibliographies and Indexes in Military Studies series. The latter will supplement my British Naval History since 1815, 1990, in the Military History Bibliographies series of Garland Publishing Company.

The dear friends of my wife, Claire, and me to whom this volume is dedicated are Neel and Iris Rich of Emory, Virginia. Our children grew up together. They have run our affairs effectively during lengthy journeys to conduct research. They have always been there when needed. We love them and thank them.

Every bibliographer is indebted to hundreds of librarians, archivists, colleagues, and friends like the Riches who have facilitated the process of acquiring access to and information about pertinent publications, journals, official documents, dissertations, and other materials. These, funding agencies, and some institutions need to be mentioned and thanked. Generous provisions for sabbatical leaves and financial assistance from the Mellon Foundation, the McConnell Fellowship, Faculty Enrichment Fund, and the Faculty Travel Grant have come from Emory and Henry College. Aid from the Virginia Foundation for Independent Colleges and the National Endowment for the Humanities have assisted in the research. Libraries in the United States and Great Britain have been used. Thanks also to the following persons: Colin Baxter, Robin Higham, John Hutcheson, Archer Jones, Thomas Morris, Jack Roper, the late George Stevenson, Jon Tetsuro Sumida, and the late Joe Thompson. Sharie Wilson puts it all together. Special thanks go to my wife Claire for her extraordinary support.

Myron J. Smith, Jr., Series Adviser, Greenwood Press, is always receptive and helpful. Mildred Vasan and Cynthia Harris, editors, Greenwood Publishing Group, have been indulgent and have assisted in numerous ways.

Abbreviations

NOTE: When there is repetition, space can be saved by the use of abbreviations. In most cases only the first name of the publisher has been included. Titles of journals, names of publishers, names of major cities often cited, and other items have been abbreviated as follows:

BIHR	Bulletin of the Institute of Historical Research
CID	Committee of Imperial Defence
diss	dissertation
ENGHISREV	English Historical Review
HISTOD	History Today
HJ	Historical Journal
JMODHIS	Journal of Modern History
JRUSI	Journal of the Royal United Services Institution
MP	Member of Parliament
NY	New York
UP	University Press
NWCR	United States Naval War College Review

Chronology

Note: All entries apply to Arthur James Balfour unless otherwise stated.

1848	25 July	Arthur James Balfour born at Whittinghame, later changed to Whittingehame, East Lothian, Scotland
1856		James Maitland Balfour, father, died
1858		To Grange School, Hoddesdon, Hertfordshire, near Hatfield House
1861		To Eton
1866		To Trinity College, Cambridge
1872		Lady Blanche, mother, died
1874		Elected MP, Hertford
1875		May Lyttelton, fiancee, died Became involved with the Society for Psychical Research
1878		To Congress of Berlin with Lord Salisbury, Foreign Minister
1879		Publication of A Defence of Philosophic Doubt Balfour elected to the Metaphysical Society

1880s		Period of the Fourth Party
1885	17 December	The famous "Hawarden Kite"
1886	8 June	Rejection of the first Home Rule for Ireland Bill
	November	Balfour to Cabinet as Scottish Secretary
	22 December	Resignation of Lord Randolph Churchill as Chancellor of the Exchequer.
1887		Balfour to Chief Secretary of Ireland, to 1891
1890s		Period of "the Souls"
1891		Death of W.H. Smith, Balfour succeeded as Leader, House of Commons and First Lord of the Treasury
1892	July	Election
1894	1 March	Gladstone resigned from his fourth government Balfour elected President of the Society for Psychical Research
1895	25 June	Joseph Chamberlain became Colonial Secretary
	July	Election
1899	9 October	War in South Africa began (sometimes called the Second Boer War)
	December	"Black Week" in Boer War
1900	September & October	Election ("Khaki" election)
1901		Balfour led Cabinet Committee to study the Education Act
1902	31 May	Boer War ended
	July	Salisbury resigned; Balfour succeeded as Prime Minister
	December	Balfour created Committee of Imperial Defence Education Act of 1902 passed Anglo-Japanese Alliance

1903	15 May	Chamberlain launched tariff reform movement
	4-16 September	Five resign from the Cabinet
1904	8 June	Winston Churchill crossed the aisle to the Liberal Party
	21 October	Incident in North Sea, Russian Baltic Fleet attacked innocent British fishing boats
		Entente cordiale, Anglo-French colonial understanding
		Balfour, President of the British Association
1905	August	Anglo-Japanese Alliance renewed
	4 December	Balfour resigned as Prime Minister
1906	January	Election; Balfour lost seat, East Manchester; Balfour first met Chaim Weizmann
	February-March	Balfour out of office, MP for City of London
1908		Balfour presented Sidgwick Memorial Lecture, Cambridge
1909	30 November	House of Lords rejected Budget
		Balfour presented Romanes Memorial Lecture, Oxford
1910	January	Election
	December	Election
1911	10 August	House of Lords passed Parliament Act of 1911
	November	Balfour retired and was replaced by Bonar Law as Leader of the Conservative-Unionist Party
1913		Balfour returned to CID
1914	January &	
	February	Gifford Lectures, Glasgow
	November	Balfour to War Council
1915	March-	
	December	Dardanelles campaign
	May	Balfour to coalition government as First Lord of the Admiralty under Asquith

1916	31 May-1 June	Battle of Jutland; Balfour formulated communique after the battle
	5 June	Kitchener died when HMS HAMPSHIRE sunk
	December	Lloyd George coalition, Balfour as Foreign Secretary
1917	April	Balfour Mission, led delegation to U.S. to borrow money, addressed U.S. Congress
	2 November	Balfour Declaration
1919	January-June	Versailles Peace Conference
1920-1921		Washington Conference; Balfour headed British delegation
1922	February	Balfour awarded Order of the Garter, Sir Arthur Balfour
	1 August	Anglo-American negotiations on war debts-reparations question; Balfour Note
		Balfour made Earl and Viscount Traprain
		Balfour presented Gifford Lectures, Glasgow
1925		Balfour as Lord President of the Council in government of Stanley Baldwin
1926		Imperial Conference - Balfour Report or Definition on constitutional structure of Dominions within the British Empire
1928	July	80th birthday, Parliament gave Balfour a Rolls Royce
1930	19 March	Balfour died at Woking; buried at Whittingehame
1931		Statute of Westminster
1962	9 May	Statute of Balfour unveiled in Member's Lobby, House of Commons

Part I
Historiographical Narrative

Chapter 1

Introduction and Biographical Essay

INTRODUCTION

Arthur James Balfour, First Earl of Balfour and Lord Traprain, is the subject of this historiographical and bibliographical survey. It is the most extensive survey of the writings by and about Balfour. It is a complete reference and research guide for the use of all levels of students and scholars and all persons interested in domestic, imperial, and international developments in the late nineteenth and early twentieth centuries. It reviews all of the important primary and secondary sources by and about Balfour.

The major features of Arthur James Balfour, 1848-1930: Historiography and Annotated Bibliography are the historiographical narrative section and the annotated bibliography section, Parts I and II. Part I, the historiographical narrative section, is a survey, chapter by chapter, of all of the important literature by and about the First Earl of Balfour. It integrates historical and biographical events, criticisms, evaluations, and observations of reviewers along with those of the author. It surveys the literature, meaning published books, monographs, official histories, government publications, memoirs, diaries, dissertations, bibliographies, pertinent articles from journals and periodicals, collections of unpublished papers and letters, various manuscripts and manuscript collections, archival and research locations and germane holdings, and published interviews, all in English and other Western languages. Fiction works, cartoons, paintings, and sculptures are also included.

There are qualitative and quantitative features of the book. A conscious effort has been made to incorporate analytical and critical judgments. In each of the chapters and subdivisions, the best, most useful, most praised works are reviewed early in the presentations, generally in some detail. Lesser, complementary, and supplementary works are included but with less emphasis and comment. Every one of the 425 numbered entries in Part II, the annotated bibliography section, is incorporated, integrated, evaluated, and placed in context in Part I, the historiographical narrative section.

Part II, the annotated bibliography section, brings together 425 entries. It is structured alphabetically so that, in most cases, the first letter of the last name of the author is the key. Each is numbered in order, 1-425. Several ways of cross-referencing, integration, linkage, and the standard indexes of author and subject have been incorporated. Every pertinent citation in Part I, the historiographical narrative section, is designated by a bracketed numbered entry, "[109]", taken from Part II, the annotated bibliography section. In addition to the two indexes at the end, there is a chronological table at the beginning.

The bibliographer and the scholar who formulate historiographical surveys of the literature on a topic face limitations. Only what has been published can be appraised and assessed. Gaps exist in that literature and further research and writing are needed. These deficiencies and opportunities for more study and publication are pointed out in the final chapter of the historiographical narrative section, Areas for Future Research.

BIOGRAPHICAL ESSAY

The Right Honourable Arthur James Balfour, First Earl Balfour and Viscount Traprain, K.G., O.M., F.R.S., F.B.A., was born in 1848 and died in 1930. Honors included the Order of Merit (O.M), the Garter (K.G.), the Earldom and Viscountcy (in 1922), and Lord President of the Council (in the 1920s). The Viscount Traprain title was named for a 35-acre, 710-foot-high mound, a laccolith caused from swelling lava, within sight of the Whittingehame estate house. It was called Traprain Law.

Arthur James Balfour was born at Whittinghame, later Whittingehame, East Lothian, Scotland, 25 July 1848. He was the eldest son and fourth child of James Maitland Balfour and Lady Blanche, daughter of the Second Marquess of Salisbury. The name "Arthur" came from the close friend of Lady Blanche, the Duke of Wellington. The Whittingehame estate was purchased in 1817, the fortune coming originally from purveying supplies to the Royal Navy in India during the Wars of the French Revolution and Napoleon.

Young Balfour attended the Eton School and Trinity College, Cambridge. At Cambridge classmates and teachers included two brothers-in-law, John Strut, Lord Rayleigh, the physicist who won a Nobel Prize, and Henry Sidgwick, the philosopher. He was a leading light in the "Apostles." His first intention was to study philosophy and become a philosopher. His interest and contributions were important if ambiguous. His works [19, 23] included A Defence of Philosophic Doubt, 1879, and Foundations of Belief, 1895.

In the 1870s he fell in love with May Lyttleton and there was serious talk of marriage, "an understanding." She died suddenly of typhoid fever in 1875. Balfour grieved for a long time and subsequently never married. He visited mediums, arranged seances, and was a spiritualist. Shortly after the death of May Lyttleton, Balfour went on a round-the-world tour.

Balfour was a founder of "the Souls." His closest friends here were the Elchos and Ettie Desborough. He was particularly close to Lady Elcho and exchanged extensive correspondence with her, recently published, edited by Jane Ridley [318].

He was said to be irresistible to women while some men saw him as a sissy and effeminate. At Cambridge he was called "Miss Balfour" and "Pretty Fanny." There were rumors of marriage to Margot Tennant who eventually married H.H. Asquith and to Consuelo Vanderbilt who married the Duke of Marlborough. This matter of his love life or lack of it elicited a variety of observations. Admiral Lord "Jacky" Fisher quipped that the "Souls" had no testicles. Lord Beaverbrook claimed "Balfour was a hermaphrodite. No one ever saw him naked."

In the 1870s after inheriting the Balfour wealth, he was among the richest young men in the kingdom. He bought 4 Carleton Gardens, a fabulous town house which featured a great curving double staircase. This elicited comment: "which to choose?," a critique of his tendency to indecisiveness.

Balfour was one of the most prominent residents of what was called the "Hotel Cecil," the name given to the powerful aristocratic family from Elizabethan days centered at Hatfield House in Hertfordshire, north of London. The Third Marquess of Salisbury, brother to Lady Blanche, was the leading Cecil. He was Foreign Secretary and then Prime Minister during the last decades of the nineteenth century until he retired in 1902, naming Balfour to succeed him. Denis Judd [208, p. 17] observed that Balfour had a "cold Cecil temperment."

Because of the Cecil aristocratic connections, Balfour has been called the last hereditary ruler of the Tory party. He was the last Prime Minister to resign without being defeated in an election; he resigned in December 1905, and the election, an overwhelming defeat of Balfour's party, was held in January 1906. Balfour remained as Leader of the Conservative-Unionist Party until 1911, two election defeats having occurred during 1910. A party revolt, identified by the motto, "Balfour Must Go!" (BMG), was successful and Bonar Law was elected Leader in 1911. [Many reminders of this precedent or unusual sequence were forthcoming in May 1997 when John Major, the Conservative Party Prime Minister and Leader of the Party, was overwhelmingly defeated by Tony Blair, Leader of the "New" Labour Party. That now makes three decisive Tory defeats in the twentieth century: 1906, 1945 when Churchill's Tories lost to the Labor Party, and 1997. Not only did Major resign as Prime Minister, to be replaced by Blair, but he also resigned the party leadership. That was unprecedented. The subsequent election for a new leader caused a serious split in the Conservative Party.]

Biographers described the demeanor of Balfour. The entry in the Dictionary of National Biography [12, pp. 41-56] saw him as "diffident and unambitious. . . always controlled his emotions. . . seemingly insincere. . . a master of debate but not a hard worker. . . nonchalance." References to the philosophical bent abounded. Denis Judd [208, pp. 15-16] noted he put on "lackadaisical airs. . . . [and was] perpetually able to see both sides of a problem." That latter characteristic infuriated critics. He frequently was accused of indecisiveness and obscurantism. The cartoonist Max Beerbohm depicted Balfour as "a wilting question mark." In a recollection in his Autobiography [17, p. xii], he described himself as "a very lazy man who has always had a job on hand."

Balfour played key, often decisive, roles in a wide variety of categories: Irish affairs, especially in the 1870s and 1880s; educational reform, especially in the Education Act of 1902; in philosophy as author of several treatises; in government as Prime Minister and holder of other Cabinet positions before and for decades after he served as Prime Minister; in defense matters as founder of the Committee of Imperial Defence; in international affairs, namesake of the Balfour Declaration, head of important delegations to the United States, and member of the Council of Ten of the Paris Peace Conference, and in imperial affairs, author of the Balfour Report or Definition which led to the constitution of the British Commonwealth of Nations.

In the 1880s, Balfour was the least active of four backbenchers, called the Fourth Party. Most prominent was Lord Randolph Churchill, father of Winston Churchill. Balfour served in a number of ministerial posts during his long career in Parliament: Secretary for Scotland, Secretary for Ireland, Leader of the House of Commons and First Lord of the Treasury, the equivalent of vice-premier under his uncle, Lord Salisbury, and then Prime Minister, 1902-1905, resigning in December 1905. The election, a spectacular victory for the Liberal Party, was held in January 1906. Balfour remained head of the Conservative-Unionist Party until 1911. He was leader of the opposition during the famous Constitutional Crisis related to the Lloyd George Budget of 1909 and culminating in the Parliament Act of 1911 which reduced the power of the House of Lords. He returned to office in the first and second coalition governments which began in May 1915, serving first as First Lord of the Admiralty and then Secretary of State for Foreign Affairs. He held that important post during the end of the First World War and, more importantly, during the peace conference at Versailles in Paris, January to June 1919. As direct assistant to Lloyd George, one of the Big Three members, he chaired the conference on occasion. Later, he served in a similar status for the League of Nations.

Balfour became a world-renowned British statesman. It is more than a cliche to state that Balfour became a household name. The Balfour "_____" was a familiar and recurring proposition. Most famous and enduring was the Balfour **"Declaration,"** the official call for a national home for the Jews in Palestine, issued in 1917. There was the Balfour **"Report"** or **"Definition,"** November 1926, during the British Imperial Conference of Dominion Prime Ministers. Balfour chaired a committee to examine the constitutional status of the United Kingdom and the Dominions, the future British Commonwealth of Nations. The committee issued the Balfour **"Report"** which defined the imperial relationship, "autonomous communities," clarifying dominion status. The ultimate result, completed after his death, was the constitution of the British Commonwealth of Nations, the Statute of Westminster of 1931.

The Balfour **"Note"** concerned intense negotiations between the United States and Great Britain in 1922. Balfour headed the British delegation to Washington to reach a settlement on the war debts/reparations question. The U.S. demanded that Great Britain repay loans made by the United States during the war. Great Britain announced that she would demand from her European allies who owed her for war loans, exactly the amount the United States demanded. This was made official with the Balfour **"Note."**

There was the Balfour **"System"** which concerned an investigation of the role and organization of aviation for the armed forces of Great Britain. The outcome was the creation of the Royal Air Force (the RAF) which took over all aviation functions and was established as a separate force, along with the Army and the Royal Navy. The latter lost its Fleet Air Arm (FAA). It was eventually returned to the Royal Navy in the late 1930s.

In addition to those official or semi-official designations connected to the Balfour name, there were other associations and a number of sobriquets. The Balfour Plan was a term used by Lord Hankey [179] in Supreme Command to describe a Balfour initiative. There were numerous nicknames: "pretty Fanny" was a nickname from classmates and colleagues when Balfour was a student at Cambridge University; "Captain Balfour" was a title placed on young Balfour in the 1870s because of his service with the Lothian and Berwickshire Yeomanry. The name was first used in the Hertford Mercury and Balfour was addressed so even in Parliament during the 1870s. "King Arthur," "High Priest," and "the Adored Gazelle" were all associated with the elite group of the 1890s, "the Souls."

Of the sobriquets, the best known was "Bloody Balfour," the derisive title aimed at Balfour when he was Secretary for Ireland. It originated because of ruthless enforcement of the Coercion Act for Ireland. Names for Balfour from Charles Stewart Parnell and the Irish nationalists proliferated: "Bloody Balfour," "Prince Arthur," "scented popinjay," "Tiger Lily," "Daddy Long Legs," and "Niminy Piminy."

Balfour was the fourth member of the Fourth Party, prominent in the House of Commons during the 1880s. Their primary function was to harrass the Liberal Prime Minister William Gladstone. Balfour was a frequent guest and close friend of Gladstone for decades, but politics eventually intervened. Gladstone, formerly a mentor to Balfour, called him "Artful Arthur."

When Balfour was Leader of the Opposition, during the constitutional crisis associated with the disposition of the Budget of 1909, "the Lloyd George Budget," David Lloyd George, then Chancellor of the Exchequer, called the House of Lords, "Mr. Balfour's Poodle." That house included a large majority of Tories and the House of Lords had continually obstructed the social and financial legislation of the Liberals since 1905; it was compliant to the wishes of Balfour, the Tory Leader.

More widely recognized was "Balfour Must Go!" (BMG), a catchy slogan devised by the influential right-wing journalist, Leo Maxse. It was taken up as the cry of disgruntled opponents within the Unionist party at the height of the constitutional crisis of 1909-1911, demanding that he step down as party leader.

The Balfour Declaration was perhaps the most significant and lasting contribution associated with Balfour, although it was not his personal declaration. It was observed that he was far sighted about the aspirations of the Jews but oblivious to the feelings and desires of the Arabs, and earlier in a similar context, the Irish. At the Versailles Peace Conference, the French Premier, Clemenceau, dubbed Balfour, "Richelieu of the Conference."

During a final visit in 1928 to King George V, Balfour resigned all of his offices. He died at Fisher's Hill, the home of his brother, Gerald, in Woking, 19 March 1930. An offer of burial in Westminster Abbey was declined. Balfour was buried at Whittingehame.

Chapter 2

Sources, Reference Works, and Histories

In the sections of this chapter, the publications, archives, and manuscript souces about Balfour will be reviewed. General and introductory works will be recommended to assist in understanding the background and context of more specific and detailed works.

SOURCES

Since Arthur James Balfour was a prominent person for several decades, from the 1870s to 1930, and since he was involved in a wide variety of international, political, philosophical, social, cultural, and literary activities, a broad survey of sources and resources to assist researchers at every level is appropriate.

British Archives: A Guide to Archive Resources in the United Kingdom with a late edition, 1995, edited by Janet Foster [130] and Sources in British Political History, edited by Chris Cook [89], 7 volumes, also recently updated, were initial places to go to learn general availability. Foster contained over 1200 listings in alphabetical order by location. All official documents, records, papers, and manuscripts of the British Government have now been moved to a central location, the Public Record Office, the equivalent of the national archives of Great Britain. All pertinent materials which might be associated with Balfour are located at Kew on the Thames near Richmond outside London. A guide to the very extensive holdings of official papers of all departments and ministries of the British government was by G.H. Martin [257]. The address: Public Record Office, Ruskin Ave., Kew, Richmond, Surrey TW9 4DU, United Kingdom.

The British Library, London, Great Russell Street, London WC1B 3DG, United Kingdom, is the equivalent of the Library of Congress where virtually every printed publication can be obtained in Great Britain. Formerly the British

Museum Library, in 1997 it moved from the famous Round Room to a new extensive location several blocks to the north. A large holding of Balfour papers can be found in the Manuscripts Division and there is an Index of Manuscripts in the British Library [195]. For Balfour, call for Additional Manuscripts 49683-49962, 280 volumes.

Cameron Hazlehurst [188] edited A Guide to the Papers of British Cabinet Ministers. It described the location, contents, and accessibility of personal papers, a result of the Political Records Project. Since Balfour was a Cabinet Minister longer than anyone, the holdings are extensive (pp.9-11).

The Balfour Papers [34] also are extensive. In addition, there is the Whittingehame collection, previously held in The Tower on the Whittingehame estate. In 1987 it was moved to the Scottish Record Office, HM General Register House, Edinburgh EH1 3YY, Scotland. Guides were Whittingehame and Strathconan Papers Handlist [36], Muniments-Handlist [35], 3529 items, and National Register of Archives (Scotland) [277], each of which described the holdings. Included were estate records, writs, legal papers, business correspondence, and personal and political letters.

Other resource centers are suggested. The archives of the Conservative Party of Great Britain [86] were deposited in the Bodleian Library, Oxford University. Included was The Tory, a newsletter and journal for party agents. The Churchill Archives, Churchill College, Cambridge University, Cambridge CB3 0DS, United Kingdom, is a relatively new and expanding center for researchers located within the college complex at Churchill College, Cambridge University. A large collection of Churchill papers are there plus others such as those of Lord Hankey. The Royal Archives, Windsor Castle, Windsor, Berkshire SL4 1NJ, United Kingdom, is the official repository for the Crown and its history. Balfour was in frequent touch, by correspondence and in residence, with the monarch, especially when he was Prime Minister and Foreign Secretary.

In addition to the major locations and archives, there are also a variety of manuscript sources about Arthur James Balfour. The Balfour Papers included materials from major centers such as the Whittingehame Collection at the Scottish Record Office and other papers at the British Library, as described above. Other manuscript sources require review. Some of these are published.

The Salisbury Papers [333], including those of the Third Marquess, are housed at Hatfield House, the ancient home of the Cecils, in Hertfordshire, north of London. Blanche Duggale wrote the official biography of Balfour and her papers [108], which included materials collected for the biography, are in the possession of Michael Dugdale. However, the reminiscences and diaries of Blanche Dugdale [105, 107] have been published. J.S. Sandars [334, 335] was Parliamentary Secretary to Balfour and his papers are deposited at the Bodleian Library, Oxford University. His memoir, Studies of Yesterday, was published.

Chaim Weizmann [401] was the most prominent Zionist leader and his papers are in the Weizmann Archives, Rehovoth, Israel.

The Chamberlain Papers [77] are in the process of being transferred to microfilm, edited by Peter Marsh. They are housed at the University of Birmingham Library. They are extensive and include the papers of Joseph, the father, and the sons, Austen and Neville. The papers of the noted journalist, J.L. Garvin [146], are available at the University of Texas Library at Austin.

Diaries, most of which have been published, were informative about the life and activities of Balfour. Among them were those of Violet Bonham Carter [55], Beatrice Webb [398], William Bridgeman, edited by Philip Williamson [416], Austen Chamberlain, edited by Robert Self [347], Viscount Reginald Esher, edited by Oliver Esher [123], W.S. Blunt [54], the Earl of Selborne [57, 344], and Baron George Riddell [317].

Two projects of publication of correspondence have created much interest and reaction from scholars and the general public. Michael Brock [63] edited the letters of Prime Minister H.H. Asquith to Venetia Stanley, a young friend, almost 700 pages. There were 560 letters from Asquith, over 300,000 words, written between 1912-1915. There were many references to Balfour. What was most sensational was the fact that they were written during the crisis leading to the war and during the war. They were filled with state and defense secrets and appeals for her advice; she was in her 20s. In May 1915 she announced her engagement to Edwin Montagu and the letters ceased. May 1915 was also the date Asquith was forced to accept the first coalition government during World War I. Jane Ridley [318] edited the correspondence between Balfour and Lady Mary Elcho, one of the Souls and a married woman with six children, Balfour, of course, being a bachelor. This correspondence was most revealing about personal feelings of Balfour. There has been much speculation about whether they were lovers. Most of the letters were exchanged between 1890 and 1915.

REFERENCE WORKS

There were a variety of helpful reference guides and aids to assist the researcher and student. A general guide was The Facts on File Encyclopedia of the Twentieth Century edited by John Drexel [103]: Balfour and the Balfour Declaration (pp. 68-69). There were two guides to the study and research of modern British history, by Larry Butler [72] and Chris Cook [88]. James Moncure [267] was the general editor of Reserach Guide to European Historical Biography, 4 volumes, the essay on Balfour by Eugene Rasor (I., pp. 104-12). Asa Briggs [62] edited the Longman Dictionary of Twentieth-Century Biography, with an essay on Balfour (p. 31). Rosemary Goring [165] edited Chamber's

Scottish Biographical Dictionary, with an essay on the Balfours (pp. 23-25). Keith Robbins [321] edited The Blackwell Biographical Dictionary of British Political Life in the Twentieth Century, with an essay on Balfour by Michael Bentley. Bentley called Balfour "a crucial transition-figure in the history of twentieth-century political life" (pp. 34-37). Stephen Koss [220] wrote an article on British political biography. Another reference source was Peter Teed [376], Dictionary of Twentieth-Century History (pp. 35-36).

A very detailed source about Arthur James Balfour is the famous Hansards or Parliamentary Debates [295] which contained verbatim transcripts of every speech in the House of Commons and House of Lords. Balfour entered the House of Commons in 1874 and moved to the House of Lords in 1922.

Certain pertinent bibliographies are cited when presenting a person and subject in the following chapters. Two general bibliographies are standards, sponsored by the Royal Historical Society and the American Historical Association: H.J. Hanham [177] and Keith Robbins [320], editors of the chronological sections for The Bibliogrpahy of British History, for 1851-1914 and 1914-1989, respectively. A total of 38,000 entries were included. Another ambitious bibliographical project of the Royal Historical Society [330] was its British Bibliographies, a database of 250,000 titles on CD-ROM, to be completed by 1997.

HISTORIES

To place Arthur James Balfour in context, several good surveys of the historical period would be useful. For Europe, the two pertinent volumes of The Rise of Modern Europe series would provide excellent background: O.J. Hale [174], The Great Illusion, up to 1914, and Bernadotte Schmitt [339], The World in the Crucible, for the war. Sir Robert Ensor [121] wrote the pertinent volume in the Oxford History of England series. Two more general surveys of the British history were by Alfred Havighurst [185, 186]. The most recent survey, Hope and Glory, in the Penguin History of Britain series, was by Peter Clarke [82].

Although he reigned only nine years, 1901-1910, King Edward VII, son of Queen Victoria, represented the period. The prewar decades in British history have become known as the Edwardian Era. Balfour was among the most notable of the Edwardians. Edward, the Edwardian Era, and the Edwardians were popular subjects for scholarly review: by Simon Nowell-Smith [288], R.J. Minney [266], Philippe Jullian [209], Piers Brendon [61], and Paul Thompson [381]. Brandon presented profiles of four representative Edwardians, Lord Northcliffe, Mrs. Pankhurst, General Baden-Powell, and Balfour (pp. 65-130), and has a new edition in paperback.

Chapter 3

Biographies and Personal Matters

BIOGRAPHIES

The universally recognized, standard biography of Arthur James Balfour has yet to be written. A number of biographical studies have been forthcoming, beginning in the 1930s with the latest effort in the mid-1980s. Elaboration on this point will be found in the final chapter, Areas for Future Research.

When Arthur James Balfour was eighty years old, in 1928, two years before his death, he commenced to write an autobiography, Chapters of Autobiography, alternate title, Retrospect: An Unfinished Autobiography, 1848-1886 [17], edited by his niece, Blanche Dugdale, and published in 1930. He dictated fifteen short chapters, covering up to 1886, and two chapters on his social life and "America, 1917," were added. He recalled his experience at the Congress of Berlin of 1878, accompanying his uncle, the Foreign Secretary, and his role in the Fourth Party. His "social life" consisted of tennis, golf, "the Souls," and music.

There are five substantial, book-length biographies of Arthur James Balfour. However, an appropriate place to begin, a concise, informative, and comprehensive survey of the life of Balfour, would be the traditional essay in the presitigious Dictionary of National Biography [12, pp. 41-56], the volume for 1922-1930. The fifteen pages is a substantial entry. The essay is by Algernon Cecil. Balfour was "philosopher and statesman," in that order. The necessary family background and education, Eton and Trinty College, Cambridge, were recounted. There followed a lengthy attempt to explain his metaphysics, closest to the philosophy of the eighteenth century Irish philosopher, George Berkeley, a philosophy of idealism. His political reputation was made in the 1870s and 1880s as Secretary for Ireland, "a personal triumph." His initiatives in creating the Committee of Imperial Defence and later involvement in defense matters were praised. He was blamed for the fiasco of the communique after the Battle of Jutland. In foreign policy, his roles in the Balfour Declaration, the Versailles Peace Conference, and the Washington Conference were highlighted.

The closest to an official biography, the "authorized" biography, was Arthur James Balfour, First Earl Balfour, 2 volumes, by his niece, Blanche Dugdale (Mrs. Edgar) [104], published in 1936. An appendix (pp. II, 413-434) described his philosophy and was written by Professor Pringle Pattison. Professor Lewis B. Namier assisted in the project. Mrs. Dugdale had access to all papers. The tone and perspective were clearly evident from the "blurb": "the most distinguished, the most discussed and least understood statesman of modern times. . . the most brilliant conversationalist of his day. . . one of the most baffling and contradictory personalities of the whole history of British politics" (introductory remarks). Extensive and intensive coverage of the political, diplomatic, international, and personal life of Balfour was incorporated. Critics have faulted it because of family inhibitions.

Such as it was, the most recent and best biography of Balfour, Balfour: Intellectual Statesman, was by Ruddock Mackay [245], published in 1985. Mackay, an academic lecturer at Dartmouth and and the University of St. Andrews, has produced biographies of Admirals Lord Fisher and Lord Hawke. The personal life of Balfour was neglected but Dugdale [104] can be utilized to fill that gap. The focus was on Balfour's contributions to the Committee of Imperial Defence, diplomatic achievements of the entente with France and with United States, the Balfour Declaration, and in reform of education. There were some gaps in the coverage and neglect in researching essential sources such as Admiralty, Foreign Office, and the Curzon papers.

Another academic, from Rutgers University, Sydney Zebel [424], published Balfour: A Political Biography, a volume in the Conference on British Studies Biography series, out in 1973. This was the third biography chronologically and touted as the first by a professional historian. Again, personal life was neglected, as were the philosophy and the psychic factors. The subtitle was fulfilled, the focus being on the long political career of Balfour, 1874 to the late 1920s, under three monarchs. Zebel saw Balfour as "the last of the Peelites" and noted that perceived enigmatic and contradictory aspects of the personality of Balfour can be explained by his determination to avoid disputes and friction, and delilberate "verbal obfuscation" (p. vii).

In 1963, before access to many of the Balfour papers was open, Kenneth Young [423], a journalist, wrote Arthur James Balfour: The Happy Life of the Politician, Prime Minister, Statesman, and Philosopher, 1848-1930, 1963. There were personal emphases, Balfour's way with women and the one major "affair," with Lady Elcho (pp. 103, 121). The Young biography has not been well received. The subtitle was off-putting. The Elcho family was much upset that Young interpreted the Mary Elcho-Balfour relationship as an "affair." They withdrew future access to the Elcho papers, removing some from the British

Library and returning them to Stanway House. Errors, for example, about the Balfour family, were noted.

The final of the five biographies of Balfour, published in 1980, was Balfour: A Life of Arthur James Balfour by Max Egremont [116], noted primarily as a politician. Some research was demonstrated and access to new sources was touted. There was better integration of the personal and political but, although explained, a continued neglect of the philosophical and the pyschic aspects. Egremont contended Balfour claimed he was identified with the Fourth Party only because he sat in a place in the House where he could stretch his long legs (p. 57). Egremont played-up Balfour as "Uncle Arthur," patriarch of an increasing extended family which spent long periods of time at Whittingehame.

A number of lesser efforts require review. The earliest endeavour was the occasion of Balfour becoming Prime Minister: Bernard Alderson [6], Arthur James Balfour: The Man and His Work, published in 1903. It was a substantial tome which reviewed his "manifold activities. . . as Statesman, Legislator, Leader, Politician, and Colleague, and in his private life as an Author and Landowner" (p. v). Edward Raymond Thompson [378], pseud., E.T. Raymond, produced a similar effort in 1920. Balfour was a balanced statesman, unlike some contemporaries who were subject to extremes such as Joseph Chamberlain, Otto von Bismarck, and William Gladstone. In 1930, Sir Ian Malcolm [250], the private secretary to Balfour, published his recollections of Balfour. He reviewed many of the events and interests of Balfour, for example, visits to the United States and interests in music, fast motor cars, tennis, and golf. Two short biographical articles appeared at the time of his death: Lord George Riddell [316] in Country Life and Winston Churchill [79] in Strand.

THE BACHELOR AND FAMILY MAN

Whittingehame, the Balfour estate in East Lothian, was orginally a compact holding of ten thousand acres, twenty miles east of Edinburgh, near Haddington. It was purchased by the grandfather, James Balfour (1773-1845), who made a fortune as a contractor for the Royal Navy in India. "The Nabob," as he was called, built a Greek-style mansion on the estate in 1820. It was a Georgian house designed by Smirke, the architect of the British Museum. The rental income during the late nineteenth century was 11,000 pounds a year. Marshall Lang [224] wrote a history of the East Lothian parish, Whittinghame. The origins were identified from artifacts such as flints, stone circles, and cairns. St. Oswald was the patron saint. The parish church was consecrated in 1245. The plot to murder Lord Darnley, husband of Mary, Queen of Scots, was planned from the estate. Catherine Snodgrass [360] wrote a history of the county of East Lothian.

A supplement to the Balfour holdings was Strathconan, an estate and shooting lodge in Rossshire in the Scottish Highlands. The inheritance of Balfour was worth four million pounds. Life in a Scottish Country House: The Story of A.J. Balfour and Whittingehame House by Paul Harris [184] described the head and the household. It was an important estate, the house having sixty rooms including thirty-three bedrooms and eight bathrooms. An advertisement in The Scotsman in 1986 set a sale price of 120,000 pounds. The author visited the area of the Whittingehame estate and interviewed the Third Earl Balfour [37] who resided in The Tower, part of the estate. The estate is now in trust and there are no direct heirs.

The value of the various holdings inherited by Balfour decreased over the next decades, apparently due to careless management, speculation, poor investments, for example on the New York Stock Exchange, and gambling. At the time of his death in 1930, there were large debts against the estate. There is a catalogue [16] for an auction of silver plate and other items of the estate of Balfour at Christie's Auction House for 16 July 1930.

The "Hotel Cecil" was the name, presumably used by jealous critics, of the powerful dynasty of aristocrats tracing origins and political power to the Tudors and continuing as the Cecil-Burghley-Salisbury nexus into the twentieth century. "Hotel Cecil" was a derisive term in reaction to the large number of Cecil relatives in official positions of government. Counting Balfour, four served as first ministers of the Crown. The mother of Balfour, Lady Blanche, was a Cecil, daughter of the Second Marquess of Salisbury of Hatfield House. Balfour was said to have "inherited" the premiership from his uncle, the Third Marquess. The Later Cecils by Kenneth Rose [324] was a family biography of the Third Marquess of Salisbury and his children. Four of the five sons entered the House of Lords. They were chiefly known for leading the campaign to ban marriage of a deceased wife's sister, claiming it was incest. They broke with Balfour later over the issue of free trade, they favored its perpetuation. "Cousin Arthur's vacillation, evasiveness, and want of principle" (p. 73) upset them. At one time Joe Thompson [380] of the University of Kentucky was preparing a biography of Lord Hugh Cecil but Thompson died in 1991.

A recent article by Janet Oppenheim [292], late of American University, was about Lady Blanche and one of her daughters, Eleanor Balfour Sidgwick, both of whom achieved prominence in a world of men. Lady Blanche, with eight children, managed two estates and launched an elementary school, Strathconan, and Mrs. Sidgwick went to Cambridge and became an official at Newman College.

Biographers make much of Balfour and May Lyttelton, daughter of George, Fourth Lord Lyttelton, and niece of William Gladstone. Balfour fell in love with her but she died. They were close to becoming engaged and her death obviously affected Balfour. He went on a world cruise and remained a bachelor. Sheila Fletcher [128] wrote a new account of the four Lyttelton girls.

Although he never married and had no children, Balfour was patriarch of the Whittingehame household, an extended family of the children of his brothers and sisters. He was generous, much beloved by his family, and was especially popular with the children. In 1907, it was noted that he drove his new motorcar around the estate at the terrifying speed of 40 miles per hour.

In the memoir of Sir Ian Malcolm [250], non-political interests and activities of Balfour were described. Balfour was widely known for his interest in classical music. Handel was his favorite composer and Balfour [26] wrote a pamphlet on Handel in the 1880s, later reprinted in The Edinburgh Review. He attended the annual Bayreuth Festival on occasion and was a friend of Richard Wagner's widow, Cosima, a notorious anti-Semite. Balfour sponsored musical events on occasion, especially those featuring Handel on the program.

For recreation, it was widely known that Balfour loved tennis and golf. Balfour enjoyed tennis, both "Real" and "Lawn," and continued to play into his seventies. He played on Centre Court, Wimbledon. Indeed, Lord Kitchener contended the the philosophical writings of Balfour were "based on this single premise: shall I be able to get out to Wimbledon in time for tennis?" (61, p. 128). He helped make golf a popular sport and he often played at the course at North Berwick. Malcolm noted that detectives were always nearby. The "first draft" of the major statue of Balfour which was to go in the House of Parliament depicted him wearing a golf hat but that was removed in the final version.

As noted Balfour had a continuing interest in the motor car. He owned a series of early ones. In 1928 the House of Commons presented him with a new Rolls Royce. He had a similar interest in aviation.

ASSOCIATIONS

In social and intellectual circles, Balfour was a participant and, in some cases, a leader, in a number of associations and social groups. Earlier, while at Cambridge in the 1860s and 1870s, Balfour was elected to the prestigious and secretive Cambridge Apostles, originally the Cambridge Conversazione Society, founded in 1820. Prominent Apostles included Alfred, Lord Tennyson, Alfred North Whitehead, Bertrand Russell, John Maynard Keynes, and Lytton Strachey. Its history was by Peter Allen [7].

More significantly, Balfour was one of the most popular and prominent members in a social group of elite aristocrats who were active during the last decade of the nineteenth century and first decades of the twentieth, the Souls. They denounced hunting and socializing. Instead, they engaged in stimulating conversation and intellectually demanding parlor games. To them, Balfour was

"King Arthur" and "the Adored Gazelle." They assembled periodically at several estate houses, including Whittingehame and Stanway. Lord Charles Beresford, more likely from the hunting crowd, named them "Souls" because all they did was sit and talk about their souls. About forty have been identified, friends and relatives in London society, including Balfours, Tennants, Lytteltons, Wyndhams, and Curzons. Aspects of the Souls were written about by Nancy Ellenberger [119], Jame Abdy [1], Angela Lambert [223], John Paterson [296], and Violet Bonham Carter [55].

Max Egremont [117], biographer of Balfour, has also written a study of W.S. Blunt and George Wyndham, cousins and both in Balfour's circle of friends. Their lives and views were quite different, pro-Irish vs. pro-Union and anti-imperialist vs. imperialist, respectively, but their friendship persisted.

An aspect of Balfour not always included in biographical and character studies was an inordinate interest in what Janet Oppenheim [293] dubbed The Other World: Spiritualism and Psychical Research in a book she wrote in 1985. Balfour, along with his brothers-in-law, Sidgwick and Rayleigh, Cambridge academics, were prominent practitioners. Balfour was elected President of the British Society of Psychical Research. Such interests prevailed in the late nineteenth century in Great Britain and the United States. The extreme case was Madame Blavatsky and the Theosophical Society, as described by Edward Hower [191] and Marion Meade [260]. Apparently an attraction of Balfour to mediums and seances was an irrational compulsion to communicate with the dead May Lyttelton. Seances were hosted at Carlton Gardens and May Lyttelton was allegedly contacted.

Chapter 4

Philosophy and Education

PHILOSOPHY

As noted, the entry on Balfour in the <u>Dictionary of National Biography</u> [12] described him as "philosopher and statesman," in that order. Balfour set out to be a philosopher and contributed several notable treatises as such. Some were published after he entered politics and he wrote and lectured on philosophy well into the twentieth century. Reactions were various.

Two works by Balfour [19, 23] on philosophy established him as a philosopher: <u>A Defence of Philosophic Doubt</u>, 1879, republished 1897 and 1920, and <u>The Foundations of Belief</u>, 1895, and with several later editions and translations into French, German, and Italian. Balfour set out to debate and resolve the perceived conflict between theology and science. He continued the debate and speculations through a series of special lectures later: in 1892, the inaugural address as Lord Rector of the University of Glasgow, "A Fragment on Progress" [24]; in 1908, the Sidgwick Memorial Lecture at Cambridge, on "Decadence"; in 1909, the Romanes Memorial Lecture at Oxford, on "Beauty and the Criticisms of Beauty"; and especially in an interrupted series, in January and February of 1914, before World War I began, the Gifford Lectures at Glasgow University, on "Theism and Humanism" [32], and a continuation delayed by the war, in 1922, on "Theism and Thought" [33].

Reactions were various. There was a Brown University dissertation, "Arthur James Balfour's Contribution to Philosophy," by C.G. Beardslee [43], completed in 1931. I.T. Noamani [287] wrote an article for <u>History Today</u>, "The Theism of Lord Balfour." Wilfrid Short [355, 356, 29], longtime private secretary to Balfour, edited a series of his non-political writings. These included extracts from some of the above philosophical writings and lectures plus observations on America, Charles Darwin, Germany, Music, and Golf. Noamani concluded Balfour was "a brilliant amateur." Rev. A. Nicholson [281] published a pamphlet containing a sermon he delivered which critiqued <u>Foundations of</u>

Belief: "a remarkable book. . . by a remarkably gifted mind" (p. 3). Karl
Pearson [297] was less impressed in his critique: "his rationalism would lead to
immorality if there is no Christian belief" (p. 6).

Lord Robert Rayleigh [309] reflected on Balfour and academic science
on the occasion of the death of Balfour. There was much praise for
contributions to science and philosophy, as a private citizen and writer, and as
a government policy-maker.

EDUCATION

The question of education and the role of government was continually
debated and legislated during the nineteenth and twentieth centuries in Great
Britain. The Church of England was the state church of Great Britain and its
role in education was prominent. Dissenters objected. Balfour was a key figure
in educational reform, especially in the last decade of the nineteenth century and
the first of the twentieth. The previous basis was the Forster Education Act of
1870 which set up board schools in urban areas. Balfour was involved in an
initiative to create a national system of primary and secondary education financed
by the localities. The role of religion was maintained. An effort in the mid-
1890s while he was leader of the House of Commons failed. After he became
Prime Minister, one of his first initiatives was a new education act, passed in
1902. It was very controversial. Balfour was credited and much praised from
many perspectives with the success. His commitment to education was
fundamental and strong.

A pertinent speech on the Bill of 1902 by Balfour [20] was published
and Balfour added remarks to a pamphlet on the Education Act of 1902 by
Morris Jones [205]. Other writings on this act and Balfour's significant
contribution were by J.E.B. Munson [273], John Roach [319], a book and article
by Eric Eaglesham [113, 114], and Sir George Kekewich [212]. A Liverpool
University dissertation by R.S. Gibson [149] was "Balfour and Education."

Another interest of Balfour, related to his philosophical inclinations, was
religious commitment. He joined the Metaphysical Society [263], founded by
Alfred, Lord Tennyson and others in 1869. The society formally opposed
agnosticism. It ended about 1880 but was revived in a comparable group, the
Synthetic Society. Balfour was seen as a guiding spirit.

In 1888, Balfour was elected to the Royal Society and in the 1920s was
offered its presidency. He was forced to decline due to other obligations. In
1904, he was elected President of the British Association and in 1921, President
of the British Academy. He received honorary degrees from most Scottish and
English universities, the University of Athens, Cracow University, and Columbia
University of New York City. He was Lord Rector of the Universities of St.

Andrews and Glasgow. He was Chancellor of Edinburgh and Cambridge
Universities.

Chapter 5

Parliament

PARLIAMENT

Arthur James Balfour entered Parliament in 1874 and died in 1930. He served several constituencies: Hertford to 1885, then Manchester East to 1906, and then the City of London. Within twelve years after entry, in 1874, he moved up to a Cabinet position, as Scottish Secretary, and the next year, more significantly, Chief Secretary of Ireland. His tenure in the Cabinet was longer than anyone else. During the 1890s he was Leader of the House of Commons and First Lord of the Treasury, effectively deputy Prime Minister to his uncle, the Third Marquess of Salisbury. Since Salisbury was in the House of Lords, Balfour spoke for the Government in the House of Commons. This was the first time the offices of Prime Minister and First Lord of the Treasury were separated. Salisbury stepped down as Prime Minister in 1902 and Balfour became Prime Minister. He resigned in December 1905, but remained as Conservative Party Leader until 1911. Even before World War I and a coalition government, Balfour returned as a member of the Committee of Imperial Defence, in 1913, and to the War Council in 1914. When the first coalition was formed, in May 1915, Balfour became First Lord of the Admiralty. In the second coalition government, December 1916, he became Foreign Secretary, holding that position into the early 1920s, during the Peace Conference and the Washington Conference. Later in the 1920s, Balfour served in a senior position, Lord President of the Council.

Obviously, the political career of Balfour was extraordinary, extraordinarily long, and extremely diverse. He moved up the "greasy pole," as Prime Minister Benjamin Disraeli earlier described the competitive process to the premiership, and served for over three years. Most Prime Ministers before and after Balfour then shifted to senior statesman status. However, circumstances, notably the war, meant that Balfour returned to ministerial office, as First Lord of the Admiralty and as Foreign Secretary, still serving two decades after he resigned as Prime Minister.   The length of his political service was unprecedented. He can be compared to Sir Thomas More, the "Man for All Seasons." His name obviously carried enormous prestige.

There were a number of political speeches of Balfour which have been published: on fiscal reform [22], on insular trade [25], and a collection of opinions and arguments [28]. There was also a book review [27] of Life of Cobden by John Morley.

While Balfour was a backbencher in the House of Commons, during the early 1880s, he gained some notoriety as a member of the Fourth Party, a ginger group most vocal during the imbroglio in the seating of Charles Bradlaugh, an avowed atheist who was elected Liberal member for Northampton.   Lord Randolph, father of Winston Churchill, was the leader; others were Sir Henry Drummond Wolff and John Gorst. Most accounts noted that Balfour was the least active of the four. The underlying objective was to embarrass and harass William Gladstone, the Liberal Leader and Prime Minister. An underlying factor was disappointment with the current leadership of the Conservative Party. Two accounts described the Fourth Party and its machinations: Harold Gorst [166] and R.E. Quinault [305], the latter calling them "enfants terribles" and "frondeurs" (p. 315).

Walter Arnstein [11] wrote the fullest account of the Bradlaugh case. Winston Churchill [80] wrote a two-volume biography of his father. Others were by Sir Robert Rhodes James [315] and R.F. Foster [131].   Recent biographies of William Gladstone were by H.C.G. Matthew [259] and Roy Jenkins [202]. Churchill wrote the biography of Lord Randolph Churchill partly to vindicate and rehabilitate him and his political reputation. "Tory Democracy" was his objective. Francis Herrick [189] has an article about Lord Randolph Churchill and the popular organization of the Conservative Party.

IRELAND

Most biographers and political analysts observing the political career of Balfour agreed that Balfour first established his reputation during the time he was Chief Secretary of Ireland, the late 1880s and early 1890s. Times were critical. The political parties of Great Britain were in transition as Joseph Chamberlain shifted from the Liberal Party to be later incorporated into the Conservative-Unionist Party. The Home Rule Bill had been defeated and many in Ireland were bitterly disappointed.   Violence in Ireland was continuing.   Two government officials were brutally murdered in Phoenix Park, Dublin. There was pressing need for reform in many areas.

When it was announced in the House of Commons that young Balfour would be the new Chief Secretary of Ireland, jeers and laughter erupted.

Balfour's policy combined coercion and reform in order, as Balfour put it, to kill the demand for Home Rule with kindness. Soon, many became impressed and, overall, the Balfour regime in Ireland gained respect from many circles. But this was also when the sobriquet "Bloody Balfour," among others, originated.

Several general surveys of Ireland in the nineteenth and twentieth century have been forthcoming: Francis Lyons [239], two by D.G. Boyce [58, 59], J. Lee [231]. The Oxford dissertation of L.P. Curtis [96] was about the Salisbury administration and Ireland. Curtis later produced two outstanding studies of the English perceptions of the Irish people as individuals; L.P. Curtis [93, 94], Anglo-Saxons and Celts and Apes and Angels.

There were excellent accounts of the tenure of Balfour as Chief Secretary. Among these were L.P. Curtis [95], Coercion and Conciliation in Ireland, Catherine Shannon [348], Arthur J. Balfour and Ireland, and Margaret O'Callaghan [290], British High Politics and a Nationalist Ireland. O'Callaghan was critical of the Balfour regime. By shifting the rhetoric to ideology, exaggerating the violence and problems, and persisting in an uncompromising stance, Balfour was responsible for reversing the advances toward Irish nationalism and eliminating a possible solution to the Irish problem. The implication was obvious: Balfour can be partially blamed for the persistence of the Irish problem, even today.

Balfour was also Chief Secretary during the spectacular political crisis-scandal associated with Charles Stewart Parnell. Parnell dominated Irish nationalist politics. Then, a major divorce scandal ultimately led to a serious split in his party. He died in 1891. Three accounts were informative: Michael Hurst [193], Jules Abels [2], and Coner Cruise O'Brien [92].

Balfour continued to be closely involved with the Irish question subsequently. A speech by Balfour [21] on Anglo-Irish financial relations was published. Richard Murphy [274] wrote an article about a later Home Rule Bill. From Cambridge University in 1968, "Arthur Balfour and the Leadership of the Unionist Party in Opposition, 1906-1911: A Study of the Origins of the Unionist Policy towards the Third Home Rule Bill," was a dissertation by J.R. Fanning [126]. Finally, there were two studies of personalities related to the Irish problem: Edward Carson by Jean Bates [41] and Walter Long by John Kendle [214]. Balfour himself wrote the introduction to the Bates piece. Balfour called Carson an old friend and colleague and credited him with "saving Ulster" (p. x) during a later crisis.

THE SALISBURY ERA

Arthur James Balfour was destined to be a philosopher when his uncle, the Third Marquess of Salisbury, enticed him to enter politics, to take a seat in the House of Commons for Hertford, the traditional home seat of the Cecils and Hatfield House. William Maehl [249] wrote a Chicago dissertation on the election of 1874, the election which Balfour won when he entered Parliament. Salisbury of the powerful aristocratic Cecil dynasty was the subject of several biographies: the first, the product of forty years of writing, four volumes plus a supplement, by his daughter, Lady Gwendolen Cecil [74, 75], Aubry Kennedy [215], most recently, Lord Robert Blake [50], and an announced forthcoming project by Andrew Roberts [322]. Salisbury was most noted for his achievements in foreign policy. That will be reviewed elsewhere. Peter Marsh [254] concentrated on the domestic statecraft of Salisbury. The Salisbury-Balfour correspondence has been published, edited by Robin Williams [415]. The correspondence was selected from seven volumes at Hatfield House and three volumes at the British Library. The correspondence covered the period from the late 1860s to 1892.

The first Cabinet position for Balfour was Scottish Secretary. The origins of that office were described by the political analyst, H.J. Hanham [178].

PRIME MINISTER

The office of Prime Minister of Great Britain has been studied by historians. Facts about the British Prime Ministers by Dermot Englefield [120] covered the office and its holders, Sir Robert Walpole of the 1740s to John Major of the 1990s, foreword by John Major. Balfour (pp. 217-22) was credited with CID and reform in education. Herbert Van Thal [392] edited a two volume survey, The Prime Ministers. Peter Clarke [83] wrote a series of essays, A Question of Leadership, reviewing the style and substance of a number of British leaders. Ironically, Balfour was seldom mentioned whereas Joseph Chamberlain, who was never Prime Minister, was highlighted and deemed the first modern politician. Similarly, A.J.P. Taylor [374] wrote a series of essays, From the Boer War to the Cold War. "Odd Man In" (pp. 55-60) was about Balfour: "a detestable man, cynical, unprincipled and frivolous." Taylor assessed the premiership as a failure despite the fact that he was responsible for CID, educational reform, the alliances with Japan and France, and later the Balfour Declaration.

The health of Salisbury declined after 1900 and he resigned as Prime Minister in 1902, anoiting his nephew as his successor. The Hotel Cecil persisted. See the several Balfour biographies about the government and administration of Balfour as Prime Minister. Sir Henry Lucy [237] wrote a history of The Balfourian Parliament. In a Columbia University dissertation, Harry Lazer [228] analyzed the political ideas and leadership of Balfour. Balfour was an aristocratic dilettante who wrote books on philosophy. As politician, he was a moderate success in education reform but an uninspiring leader. The handling of the free trade-tariff reform debate split the party and the defeat of 1906 was one of the worst political disasters of modern British history. "Unionist Politics and the Aftermath of the General Election of 1906," by David Dutton [112], was about an apparent struggle of control of the party between Balfour and Chamberlain. Of the 157 Unionist members returned, 109 were Chamberlainites, 32 for Balfour, and others. But the position of Balfour should not be underestimated.

The work of Geoffrey Searle [342, 343] was pertinent to the period of the Edwardian crisis. One significant study focused on the "national efficiency" movement, mostly the initiative of Liberal Imperialists, an influential right-wing arm of the Liberal Party. The issues were related to Balfour: education reform, the Committee of Imperial Defence, and reform of the poor law. A second work was Corruption in British Politics, for example, stock-jobbing, honors trafficking, patronage, and the armaments trust. Great Britain avoided major political scandals such as Panama in France and Tammany Hall in the United States. Balfour was involved in honors trafficking and potential conflicts of interest since he held sixty directorships of companies when he took office in 1902. He personally lost one thousand pounds in a stock market collapse (pp. 44-47).

As Prime Minister and later as Cabinet Minister, Balfour served under two monarchs. The biography of King Edward VII was by Sir Sidney Lee [232], 2 volumes; that of George V by Sir Harold Nicolson [283].

THE CONSTITUTIONAL CRISIS

The most important constitutional crisis of the twentieth century played itself out in the period between 1909 and 1911. Not in power but leader of the opposition, Balfour was a major participant in the crisis. He had resigned in December 1905 as Prime Minister and the Liberals won a major victory in the election of January 1906. However, the Unionists maintained a large majority in the House of Lords. As Unionist Leader, Balfour orchestrated a consistent process of obstruction of a series of Liberal bills, mostly social reform measures. The Liberal Party, first led by Henry Campbell-Bannerman and then Henry Asquith, introduced an ambitious program of social reforms. These matters were reviewed by Michael Craton [90] and Alan Russell [332]. Jose Harris [183] has an article on Campbell-Bannerman; Cameron Hazlehurst [187] an article and Stephen Koss [219] and Roy Jenkins [201] biographies of Asquith. An idiosyncratic but classical explanation of the political consequences affecting their party was The Strange Death of Liberal England by George Dangerfield [97], noted primarily as an American historian.

The constitutional tradition was that all money bills were initiated in the House of Commons and the House of Lords did not significantly tamper with them. By 1909, there were two sectors of the budget requiring increase, social reform and naval expansion. The Liberal Chancellor of the Exchequer, David Lloyd George, drew up a radical budget for 1909 which introduced a series of new taxes, for example, on land values and inheritance. He called it "the People's Budget." Dukes cost the government more than DREADNOUGHTS, Lloyd George quipped.

In an unprecedented move, the House of Lords voted to reject the Budget of 1909. The death of King Edward VII caused delay. The result was two elections in 1910, in January and December. Neither election was a clear mandate. The Liberals then passed the Parliament Act of 1911 in the House of Commons. It effectively removed the veto on legislation of the House of Lords. Would the House of Lords pass the bill? There was some confused discussion about the king appointing hundreds of new peers. In the end the Lords passed the bill.

Since these events were so important politically, there was an extensive literature. It was this crisis that caused Lloyd George to describe the House of Lords as "Mr. Balfour's Poodle," the title of the account of the crisis by Roy Jenkins [203]. A history of the House of Lords from the early seventeenth century to 1911 was by Clyve Jones [204]. Andrew Adonis [5], in the Oxford Historical Monographs series, described the peerage and the political system in effect during this period. Klaus Epstein [122], later a noted German historian, wrote his Harvard University dissertation on the constitutional crisis, subsequently published by Garland Publishers. Frank Hardie [182] wrote an article, "The King and the Constitutional Crisis." Lord Salisbury formulated a rationale for the continued constitutional role of the House of Lords, called the referendal theory, as explained by Corinne Weston [405]. The two elections of 1910 were the focus of a book by Neal Blewett [52]. Christopher Silvester [358] recounted an episode during the crisis: when Prime Minister Herbert Asquith announced that the king had agreed to appoint five hundred peers if necessary, an organized chant of "traitor" persisted for half an hour. In the end 113 peers voted against the Parliament Act. They were called "diehards" and their history was by Gregory Phillips [302]. Lloyd George's People's Budget was the subject of a work by Bruce Murray [275].

Walter Bagehot [14], the great British constitutional historian, wrote The English Constitution originally in 1867, frequently reprinted. The 1928 edition in the World's Classics series, contained an introduction by Balfour, signed from Whittingehame, November 1927. He reviewed the national and international circumstances at the time of the original publication. He compared American and British political systems, explaining the differences, for example, that Great Britain had no written constitution.

Chapter 6

The Party and the Press

THE CONSERVATIVE-UNIONIST PARTY

Most histories of the Conservative Party begin in the 1830s. The subject has attracted much interest. A large number of surveys, many published in the 1990s, have appeared. Lord Robert Blake [49] has made himself the foremost authority on that history, especially with The Conservative Party, originally the Ford Lectures of 1968 at Oxford University. The subtitle then was Peel to Churchill, since updated in the revised editon of 1985, Peel to Thatcher. The chapter incorporating the Balfour administration was entitled "Defeat and Recovery" (pp. 167-200). Longman Publishers have recently announced a five volume history of the Conservative Party, 1830-1975 [190]. The entire tenure of Balfour was covered in volumes already published: Richard Shannon [349], The Age of Disraeli, Richard Shannon [350], The Age of Salisbury, and John Ramsden [306], The Age of Balfour and Baldwin. Donald Southgate [362] collected a series of essays about leaders of the Conservative Party, that on Balfour by Alfred Gollin.

More histories of the party in the twentieth century have been published: Anthony Seldon [345], Brendan Evans [124], Martin Francis [132], John Fair [125], Stuart Ball [38], Jeremy Smith [359], and John Charmley [78]. Charmley has made a name as a revisionist historian. He wrote of "Balfourian dog days." Studies of conservatism in British history were by Anthony Seldon [346] and Robert Eccleshall [115]. Seldon edited essays, How Tory Governments Fall, covering the period since 1783; the essay on the Balfour regime was by Martin Pugh (pp. 189-230). Balfour inherited a dubious political legacy from Salisbury and he avoided the vulgar side of politics. He appeared to be detached and aloof and lost creditability during the free trade-tariff reform debate. Pugh also entitled a chapter, "The Strange Death of Conservative England" (pp. 223-30). Interestingly, Balfour was ignored by Eccleshall who reviewed conservatism since the sixteenth century. Included were Edmund Burke, Robert Peel,

Benjamin Disraeli, Baron Balfour of Burleigh, Harold Macmillan, and, of course, Margaret Thatcher.

A case can be made that Joseph Chamberlain, the popular Birmingham politician, completely disrupted the political party structure of Great Britain, not once, but twice. To proceed, an explanation about party names requires review. Histories of the Conservative Party of Great Britain, the party that has been in power the most number of years in modern times, begin with the year 1830. "Tories" was and is their popular name. After the demise of the Whig Party, the Liberal Party was the other party during the nineteenth century, the party of William Gladstone. In the mid-1880s Gladstone came out openly for Irish Home Rule. Joseph Chamberlain, a rising member of the Liberal Party, opposed that and he and some others withdrew support, winding up joining the Conservatives in the next decade. The name Unionist Party was adopted, meaning the party favored continued union with Ireland. Chamberlain served as Colonial Secretary in the Salisbury and Balfour administrations. Then, in 1903, Chamberlain publicly came out against free trade, or what he and powerful supporters called tariff reform. Again, party structures were disrupted. Longtime "free traders" found themselves isolated. Again, a party split ensued, this time, the Unionist Party. Balfour was in the middle, and, to some extent, the victim, of the second Chamberlain initiative. The Labor Party was a twentieth-century phenomenon, first gaining political recognition in the election of 1906. It later surpassed the Liberals in the interwar period.

The 4000 page official biography of Joseph Chamberlain was thirty-seven years in the making, the first three volumes by J.L. Garvin [145] and the second three by Julian Amery. Most helpful was the new bibliography on Chamberlain by Scott Newton [280] in Greenwood's Bibliographies and Indexes in World History series. Subsequently, at least a biography each decade has appeared: by Peter Fraser [134], by Richard Jay [199], and, most recently, by Peter Marsh [255]. Titles of reviews were informative: "From Screw King to Wirepuller" and "Was Joseph Chamberlain the best Prime Minister we never had?" The title of an essay by David Dutton [111] was "Life Beyond the Political Grave: Joseph Chamberlain, 1906-1914." Chamberlain was seriously injured in a carriage accident in 1903, suffered a debilitating stroke in 1906, and died in 1914.

The new Marsh biography of Chamberlain was another example of the continuing interest in Edwardian era politics. A 1996 contribution to the British History in Perspective series was by David Powell [304], The Edwardian Crisis. David Brooks [64] dubbed the period The Age of Upheaval and pointed out that Chamberlain was the most commanding figure in the ranks of the Unionists. Balfour squandered a substantial political inheritance. More prolific has been E.H.H. Green [168, 169] who has just produced two books about British politics, 1880-1914, entitled The Age of Transition and The Crisis of Conservatism.

Green noted that George Dangerfield [97] wrote the classic, The Strange Death of Liberal England. He was wrong, the period in question was a crisis of Conservatism, Green contended. In his own essay, "The Strange Death of Tory England," Green [170] noted the party suffered three election defeats in a row and engaged in a fratricidal struggle during the Edwardian era. The late Joe Thompson [379] and Frans Coetzee [84] also have contributed studies on Edwardian conservatism.

The ultimate issue within the Unionist Party after 1903 was free trade vs. tariff reform, so distracting that it split the party. The Liberals enjoyed a spectacular victory in 1906. Balfour's Burden: Arthur Balfour and Imperial Preference by Alfred Gollin [158], Unionists Divided: Arthur Balfour, Joseph Chamberlain and the Unionist Free Traders by Richard Rempel [314], and Tariff Reform in British Politics by Alan Sykes [370] were three monographs covering the debate. Sykes noted that it engulfed the party until 1913 when Home Rule displaced it as the ultimate issue in politics. Shorter accounts were by Peter Fraser [137], Neal Blewett [51], and two contemporaneous works by George Peel [298, 299]. The Blewett piece was entitled "Free Fooders, Balfourites, Whole Hoggers: Factionalism within the Unionist Party."

A recent dissertation from the University of Minnesota by Larry Witherell [421] focused on an anti-Balfour, tariff reformer, Henry Croft. Croft came from the radical right, a group elaborated upon by Alan Sykes [369], Barbara Farr [127], and George Boyce [57]. Boyce edited the papers of the Second Earl of Selborne, First Lord of the Admiralty under Salisbury and Balfour. Selborne dubbed the opponents of the Unionists the "Home-Rule-Pro-Boer-Little-Englander-Socialist Party" and the Parliament Bill of 1911 the "Emasculation of the House of Lords and Establishment of the House of Commons as a Single Chamber Tyranny Bill" (p. x).

What was Prime Minister Balfour (until 1905) and Party Leader Balfour (until 1911) doing during this Edwardian crisis in conservatism and the split in the Unionist Party? For one thing, according to R.B. Jones [206], he reorganized the administrative structure of the Party, creating a professional bureaucracy so well established that it was immune to manipulation by pressure groups, even the powerful organization accumulated by Joseph Chamberlain. But there was also the powerful and ultimately successful "Balfour Must Go!" (BMG) movement. He was forced out as party leader. This was described by David Dutton [110], Peter Fraser [138], and Mary Langan [225]. Meantime, the great constitutional crisis was proceeding. That is reviewed elsewhere under "Parliament."

THE PRESS

Many of the biographical and character studies of Balfour cite a statement he frequently made: he never read newspapers, as if they were an annoyance and were not to be taken seriously. That makes another aspect much remarked about concerning Balfour even more ironic: that he maintained close, often secret, contacts with journalists and was generous in giving certain ones exclusive access to policy decisions in politics, defense matters, and international relations. This was the formative period of the rise of sensational or "yellow" journalism and also the age of powerful editors. Examples were W.T. Stead of the Pall Mall Gazette, J.L. Garvin of The Observer, C.P. Scott of the Manchester Guardian, Charles a'Court Repington of The Times, Leopold Maxse of the National Review, J.A. Spender, John St. Loe Strachey of The Spectator, Spencer Wilkinson, and A.G. Gardiner of the Daily News. Later, during the 1920s and 1930s, it was the age of powerful proprietors such as Lords Northcliffe, Rothermere, and Beaverbrook.

Balfour was especially close to Admiral Lord Jacky Fisher, First Sea Lord of the Admiralty during the first two decades of the twentieth century. Balfour, Fisher, Joseph Chamberlain, Lloyd George, and Winston Churchill all became notorious for close dealings with and manipulation of the press. An outstanding example related to Balfour was the case of C.P. Scott of the Manchester Guardian. Scott was increasingly interested in and drawn to the Zionist position, became a close contact with Chaim Weizmann, and first brought Weizmann to the attention of Balfour and Lloyd George. A direct result was the Balfour Declaration, covered in detail in a separate chapter below. J.L. Garvin and The Observer enjoyed enormous influence during the Budget-House of Lords crisis, 1909-1911, in what would now be called high politics. The tariff reform vs. free trade debate was another issue attracting politicians and journalists in close collaboration, especially Balfour and Joseph Chamberlain.

The literature on these matters was expansive. A general introduction would be Dennis Griffiths [173], The Encyclopedia of the British Press, which presented essays by experts covering chronological periods, for example, 1800-1860 and 1860-1918. The best scholarly general study, The Rise and Fall of the Political Press in Britain, with a volume on the nineteenth and a second volume on the twentieth century, was by the late Stephen Koss [222]. Koss described a systematic process of manipulating the political press to formulate party programmes, to implement political strategies, and to serve personal ambitions. Others with general coverage of this topic were Joel Wiener [411], Alan Lee [230], and James Startt [363]. An older, classical study by the late Oran Hale [175] stressed the influence of yellow journalism contributing to the deterioration of relations between the British and Germans before World War I. The

Scaremongers was the title of a study by A.J.A. Morris [272] about powerful press leaders such as Northcliffe and Repington promoting an image of an evil and expansionist Germany. An article by J.M. McEwen [242] and an Oxford dissertation of 1971 by Stephen Inwood [196] focused on the press in politics in Great Britain during the war.

There were numerous case studies of pertinent individual newspaper editors and proprietors. C.P. Scott and the Manchester Guardian was covered by J.L. Hammond [176]. J.L. Garvin and The Observer has attracted more interest: Alfred Gollin [160], David Ayerst [13], Joanna Anstey [10], and Marion Miliband [265]. Garvin was particularly powerful and influential over several decades. Another powerful and influential editor was W.T. Stead and the Pall Mall Gazette: Frederic Whyte [410], Raymond Schults [340], and Harvey Blumenthal [53]. Joseph Baylen [42] is preparing a biography of Stead. Other individual studies were as follows: J.M. Scammell [338] on Spencer Wilkinson, John Hutcheson [194] on Leopold Maxse, H. Bralley [60] on John St. Loe Strachey, Stephen Koss [221] on A.G. Gardiner, and Keith Wilson [420] on The Morning Post.

One of the best known and most powerful of the proprietors was Max Aitken, a native of Canada who came to Great Britain and purchased several newspapers, subsequently gaining official office, and raised to the peerage as Lord Beaverbrook. Concerning this period, Beaverbrook [44, 45] himself authored Politicians and the War, in 2 volumes, and Men and Power. In the latter, Beaverbrook observed that Balfour "didn't believe in anything or any body" (p. xi). Peter Fraser [135] has a piece which specifically refuted Politicians and the War. Much was lies and speculation. Accounts about Beaverbrook were by A.J.P. Taylor [373] and Anne Kelsch [213].

Chapter 7

The Balfour Declaration

The name of Arthur James Balfour, deserved or not, will always be directly linked and best known because of an official action of the British Government in November 1917. The time was toward the end of World War I. The Allies seemed to be winning but the situation was in flux, especially in the Middle East, then controlled by the Ottoman Empire, one of the Central Powers. On the other side, the Allies, Great Britain, France, Russia, and Italy had already agreed, in a series of "secret treaties," to divide up much enemy territory into spheres of influence. The pertinent agreement in this case was the Sykes-Picot Agreement of 1916. The negotiators were Sir Mark Sykes for Great Britain and Francois-Georges Picot for France. Among other things, it provided for the postwar division of the Ottoman Empire into British and French spheres of influence.

The British were concerned about a number of issues: the future security of the Suez Canal, access to India, the Russian Revolution, the disposition of Jews in Russia, attracting the Americans to participate in the postwar arrangements, continued access to oil of the Middle East, elimination of the Turks, and excluding German influences. There was fear that the Germans might preempt British initiatives. The headquarters of international Zionism at that time was in Berlin. So, not only were there German and Russian considerations, but also there were concerns about legitimate interests of the French, the Americans, the Italians, the Arabs, and even the Pope. At the time a British military force was conducting operations against the Turks and Germans in the region. General Edmund Allenby led a British force which captured Jerusalem and the area of Palestine. The British believed rectifications to Sykes-Picot were essential. In fact, after the war, Great Britain was awarded the Mandate of Palestine.

The Cabinet discussed these issues frequently over several years. A decision was made to issue an official statement. The statement most threatened the future existence of the Ottoman Empire. There seemed to be less concern about the Arabs who inhabited the territory in question at the time. The statement was purposely made to be ambigious. It was studiously vague. It was a political, not a legal, statement. Some say it was actually aimed at Europe, not the Middle East.

The statement approved by the British Cabinet immediately became linked with the signature at the end. Curiously, the official statement was in the form of a letter to Lord Rothschild, the recognized leader of the numerous and powerful Jewish community within Great Britain. Another irony was that the majority of Jewish community in Great Britain did not approve of the position of the Jewish group pressuring for the British support. Most British Jews were proud of their Britishness and feared the Zionist aim would jeopardize that which they had achieved.

The statement became known as the Balfour Declaration; Balfour was Foreign Secretary at the time, and he signed for the Cabinet. The Jewish group, representing a minority of British Jewry, was called the Zionists. Since the 1890s, the international Zionists had urged creation of a nation state for the Jews in Palestine which they saw as their ancient and rightful home. The primary spokesperson in Great Britain for Zionism was Dr. Chaim Weizmann, a Jewish scientist from Manchester. Weizmann was later to be the first President of the State of Israel when it was created in 1948.

Upon the return of Arthur Balfour and the British delegation from the official visit to the United States in the spring of 1917, the British Cabinet finally resolved to take an initiative which would dramatically affect the political and international situation in the Middle East, preempt any German initiatives, and appease Jewish hopes and objectives. Actually, while Balfour was in the United States, he had met Judge Louis Brandeis and his secretary, Felix Frankfurter, two of the most prominent Jewish leaders among a powerful and influential Jewish community in America. They were urged to gain support from President Woodrow Wilson of the United States. Later, that was forthcoming.

The Cabinet reached a decision to support the Zionist position. The Balfour Declaration was in fact an official letter from Balfour, the Foreign Secretary of Great Britain, to Lord Rothschild, prominent leader of British Jews, dated 2 November 1917. The Declaration was carefully worded to encourage the Jews but not upset the Arabs. The key phrase was "national home," rather than a state or nation for the Jews, and not encroaching upon the native Arabs. The French, Americans, and Italians had indicated support. The addressee of this curious diplomatic ploy was Lord Walter Rothschild, the current head of the British Rothschilds. The history of the English Rothschilds was written by Richard Davis [98].

The authorized biographer of Balfour, his niece Blanche Dugdale [106], wrote a short explanation of the background of the Declaration on the tenth anniversary of the death of Balfour, in 1940. The standard account was by Leonard Stein [364], himself an official of the Zionist organization. The several drafts produced during the summer and fall of 1917 were each described in detail. The reason the Declaration was addressed to Lord Rothschild was that the official headquarters of the Zionist organization was in Berlin. The British Foreign Office obviously could not convey the document there.

As might be expected, other accounts of the Balfour Declaration have been published: by Ronald Sanders [336], by Joseph Jeffries [200], by Herbert Sidebotham [357], in Hebrew by N.M. Gelber [147], in French by Renee Neher-Bernheim [278], two works by Mark Levene [234, 235] who credited Mark Sykes and Lucien Wolf, by Edwin Montagu [271] who opposed the Declaration, by David Fromkin [143] who called it the peace to end all peace, and by Conrad Grieb [172] who called it a "warrant for genocide" (the subtitle). Two books written about 1940 referred to the promised land and the Jewish national home, respectively by Norman Bentwick [48] and Paul Goodman [164]. Two impressive articles, of 1970 and 1992, described the Declaration and its makers, respectively by Mayir Verete [393] and Jehuda Reinharz [310]. 50th anniversary commemorations were written by Jon Kimche [218], stressing the great powers, and Richard Lebow [229], stressing the role of Woodrow Wilson.

The background for British interests in the Middle East and in Palestine has been extensively explained. A recently published overview of the general situation in the Middle East during and after the First World War was produced by Marian Kent [216]. An impressive and productive entree would be the rare bibliography, William Olson [291], Britain's Elusive Empire in the Middle East, 1900-1921, containing 664 annotated entries, most published since 1950. Next, go to Isaiah Freidman [142], The Question of Palestine, 1914-1918: British-Jewish-Arab Relations, with a second edition, 1992. Friedman stressed the propaganda factor and Britain's determination to preempt the Germans, to literally outbid the Germans as related to attracting Russian, Jewish, and American support. Other surveys were as follows: Elie Kedourie [210], England and the Middle East, John McTague [248], British Policy in Palestine, Elizabeth Monroe [270], Britain's Moment in the Middle East, Jukka Nevakivi [279], Britain, France and the Arab Middle East, and the older Bible and Sword: England and Palestine from the Bronze Age to Balfour, by the late prolific popular historian, Barabara Tuchman [388]. Monroe stressed the place of oil in the complex mix of issues. McTague gave maximum credit to Herbert Samuel, a Jewish member of the Cabinet who articulated the ultimate British position as early as 1914. There was a recent biography of Samuel by Bernard Wasserstein [397]. Tuchman stressed religion, Palestine being the holiest spot in the world. Martin Gilbert [151] has just produced a pertinent survey, Jerusalem in the Twentieth Century. A new innovative interpretation of these issues incorporating economic factors was Roger Adelson [3], London and the Invention of the Middle East: Money, Power, and War, 1902-1922. There were three British goals: security of the lifeline to India and Asia, control of the oil reserves, and maintenance of primary influence in the area. The German threat was more important than Jewish or Arab nationalism. Adelson [4] also wrote a biography of Mark Sykes, the British negotiator in preliminary arrangements.

Most agree that the interests of the Arabs remained a low priority. British-Arab relations were reviewed by John Glubb [155], A.L. Tibawi [383], Eliezier Tauber [372], Elie Kedourie [211], and Bruce Westrate [406]. Westrate described the role of the British Arab Bureau, headquartered in Cairo. The most noted operative from the Arab Bureau was T.E. Lawrence, Lawrence of Arabia, advocate for the Arabs. Lawrence [226, 227] himself elaborated on his disappointments in Revolt in the Desert and, more popular, The Seven Pillars of Wisdom. An article by A.L. Tibawi [384] described a failed initiative by Lawrence to conclude an Arab Balfour Declaration. A major purpose of the Arab Bureau was gathering of intelligence for imperial and military purposes. That aspect was reviewed by Anthony Verrier [395] and Yigal Sheffy [353]. A survey of Arab nationalism as a movement was by Muhammad Muslih [276].

Based on the final results, the British obviously favored the Jewish position, and, within the Jewish position, the most extreme demand. Zionism was an international Jewish movement founded in the 1890s and advocating an exclusive and national state for international Jewry. The literature on British-Zionist relations was expansive, much of it focused on the most important Zionist leader in Great Britain, Dr. Chaim Weizmann. The most extensive source materials on Zionism can be found in the Zionist Archives [425] in Jerusalem. Nahum Sololow [361] wrote a two-volume history of Zionism published in 1919. Balfour wrote the preface. In it, he described his early meetings with Weizmann. Subsequently, there was a three-volume history by David Vital [396]. Vital described the surprising situation: "the British government embarked on an unprecedented political relationship with a small, self-appointed, and in many ways unrepresentative body of Jewish notables" (III., p. 221). Balfour's [31] speeches on Zionism have been published.

A series of articles by Mayir Verete [394], From Palmerston to Balfour, stressed diplomatic activities. For Balfour it was the Balfour Declaration which was the focus of several essays (pp. 1-38, 204-26). Verete contended the Declaration was at the initiative of the government, not the Zionists. The government sought out the Zionists because of a need to reconcile the interests of allies, France, Russia, and the U.S.

The Jewish-British background was supplied by W.D. Rubinstein [331]. British-Zionist relations were reviewed by Frank Hardie [181] and D.Z. Gillon [153]. Most influential and contributory in the formative process leading to the Balfour Declaration was the Zionist leader in Great Britain, Chaim Weizmann. With the persistent support and sponsorship of C.P. Scott, editor of The Manchester Guardian, Weizmann began lobbying for the Zionist position shortly after he moved to Great Britain in 1904. He met frequently with the most influential British leaders including Balfour and Lloyd George.   His autobiography [400] was entitled Trial and Error. Two recent and extensive biographies were by Norman Rose [326] and Jehuda Reinharz [311]. The third volume of the Reinharz study is forthcoming. Chapter 6 of the second volume was on the Balfour Declaration (II., pp. 172-212). Reinharz [312, 313] also authored two articles on Zionist activities of Weizmann. Three short works on Weizmann merit notice. Leonard Stein [365, 366] praised Weizmann before the Jewish Historical Society and in the Weizmann Memorial Lecture, both in 1964. In an earlier Weizmann Memorial Lecture, in 1955, the renowned diplomatic historian, Charles Webster [399], praised Weizmann's accomplishment as "the greatest act of diplomatic statesmanship of the First World War" (p. 14).

Jews and Zionists increasingly glorified Balfour after 1917. He visited Palestine in the 1920s and spoke before Jewish audiences. Balfour was frequently praised and memorialized before and after his death.

Chapter 8

Defense, Empire, and Diplomacy

Arthur James Balfour was minister for Scotland, minister for Ireland, Leader of the House of Commons and First Lord of the Treasury, Prime Minister, and Lord President of the Council during his political career. These offices were noted primarily for their domestic activities. Balfour also served lengthy terms as First Lord of the Admiralty and Foreign Secretary and he chaired international conferences and delegations. He signed the Balfour Declaration, the Balfour Note, the Balfour Definition, and the Balfour System, all of which involved foreign affairs. Earlier chapters concerned domestic activities. This chapter focuses on colonial and international aspects.

DEFENSE

The area of education was a special contribution of Arthur James Balfour. So was imperial defense. Balfour has been identified significantly with originating the modern strategic and defense structure of the British Commonwealth. The institution involved was the Committee of Imperial Defence (CID), the first formal effort at coordination and joint action of naval and military forces and overall strategy, later even including imperial forces. This led to the war planning process. As Prime Minister, Balfour created it in its modern form in 1902, and, beginning in 1903, he took over as chair and sustained his interest and participation, as Prime Minister, and later in appropriate Cabinet positions for the rest of his political career.

A number of factors influenced the changes leading to coordinating imperial defense and strategic or war planning. The Prussians-Germans created the military general staffs and executed highly successful war plans in the 1860s, culminating in the Franco-Prussian War of 1870-1871 and the unification of Germany. Some British colonies were maturing and demanded a role, for example, Canada, Australia, and New Zealand. Significant expansion in the naval and military forces was anticipated. The beginnings of the system of alliances meant more obligations and responsibilities, for example, with Japan, France, and Russia. And the alarmingly poor performance of British forces in the Boer War caused concern. During the war Great Britain was condemned and threatened by groups of countries, for example, Germany, France, and the Netherlands. Special concern was demonstrated about India and unobstructed access to it.

Prior to 1902, some ad hoc colonial defense committees had met on occasion and staff structures for the armed forces were considered. Balfour was credited with taking the most important initiative when he formed the Committee of Imperial Defence in 1902. He followed up that action by attending the meetings and taking over as chair.

The definitive study of these matters was Defending the Empire by Rhodri Williams [413]. It was the first scholarly analysis. Balfour and the Unionists laid the foundations and, even in opposition later, continued to participate and support further reforms and improvements. Balfour served on CID before and during World War I. Some products of these efforts were the DREADNOUGHT revolution and the army reforms identified with Richard Haldane. The Origins of Imperial Defence by Norman Gibbs [148] elaborated on these matters. Essays collected by Ian Beckett [46], Politicians and Defence, covered these and later developments.

Three dissertations and an article were informative on the background and origins: Donald Schurman [341] for Cambridge University who explained the change from colonial to imperial defense, William McDerott [240] for Toronto who traced the organizational changes from 1871 to 1907, Rhodri Williams [414] for Oxford who stressed the contribution of Balfour, and Nicholas D'Obrain [289] in The Journal of the Royal United Services Institute who described the participation of Winston Churchill just before the war. In addition to Balfour and Churchill, government ministers, organizational and bureaucratic initiatives were taken by Sir George Clark, Lord Maurice Hankey, and Lord Reginald Esher. Their contributions were recounted by John Gooch [163] and Hankey [179] himself. Biographical studies of Esher were by Peter Fraser [136] and James Lees-Milne [233] and of Hankey, in three volumes plus an article, by Stephen Roskill [327, 328]. The result of these structures were military and naval staff organizations and formal war planning for Great Britain. John Gooch [161, 162], in two works, and Sir William Jackson [198] wrote on these processes and their maturation. Associated reforms of the army were described by Bryce Poe [303] and, beginning in 1909, air power was incorporated, described by Alfred Gollin [159].

Over and above the foundation of CID and service on it while in office and in opposition, Balfour was closely identified with and an active supporter in and out of office of the Royal Navy. Balfour brought Hankey in to administer

CID. He also collaborated with Admiral Lord "Jacky" Fisher who implemented an expansive series of reforms of the Royal Navy, including DREADNOUGHT, the innovative battle cruiser, reorientation of the fleets, and significant personnel improvements. Later, during the war, Balfour and Fisher were instrumental in creating the Board of Invention and Research, a contribution described by Roy MacLeod [247]. The definitive source on these was Arthur Marder [253], From DREADNOUGHT to Scapa Flow, 5 volumes. Robert Massie [258] wrote a sensationalized book featuring Fisher, Balfour, and some of these matters. Rhodri Williams [412] was best at summarizing the role of Balfour, Fisher, and naval reform. Ruddock Mackay [246] has the best biography of Fisher. An extensive bibliography on the Royal Navy was by Eugene Rasor [308].

In the first coalition government, May 1915-December 1916, Balfour was brought in as First Lord of the Admiralty. The Dardanelles fiasco was being exposed and Fisher resigned. Under crisis circumstances, a prestigous minister was needed. Balfour's service as minister was generally undistinguished. He was First Lord when the most important naval battle of the war, Jutland, on the last day of May and first day of June 1916, was fought. That battle was recounted by N.J.M. Campbell [73], J.J. Irving [197], and Volume III of Marder [253], the only one of the five to be updated with a new edition. A bibliography on the battle was by Eugene Rasor [307].

Balfour was the object of criticism, not so much about the battle, but about the public announcement of its results. Balfour wrote the first British communique immediately after the battle of Jutland. The Germans immediately issued a communique declaring victory and claiming dozens of British ships were lost. By contrast, the British communique was brief, uninformative, and pessimistic. A major controversy ensued and he was personally blamed. He contended that he included the maximum information known at the time, prior to the arrival back to bases of the British fleet. A journalist critic concluded: "Never was a thing so badly handled" [116, Egremont, p. 273]. Winston Churchill, a former First Lord, was solicited to write a supplementary, more informed, and more appropriate announcement. An excellent source for this, the battle, and, indeed, the war was The World Crisis, 6 volumes, by Winston Churchill [81]. The standard and official biography of Churchill was by Martin Gilbert [152], 8 volumes. An unfinished biography of Churchill, but covering this early period, was by Peter de Mendelssohn [262].

Another incident which occurred while Balfour was First Lord was less important, but the account of it by Alan Coles [85] was grossly exaggerated. Coles contended it prolonged World War I, influenced the rise of Hitler, and was a cause of World War II! The incident was the attack on the German U-boat, U-27, which was sunk. The eleven German survivors were murdered. Coles blamed the Admiralty and also accused it of cover-up.

EMPIRE

The British Empire was the largest in the world; "the sun never set..." It was the hegemonic power of the world from the late eighteenth and through the nineteenth centuries; the "Pax Britannia." In the twentieth century, changes and structural rectifications necessarily were made. There were various statuses: condominiums, chartered territories, protectorates, crown colonies, mandates, and India. Some advanced colonies matured into Dominion status and the Dominions pressured for a more federated structure, the British Commonwealth of Nations. Excellent background information on these matters was presented by A.P. Thornton [382] and Richard Shannon [351].

The continuing role of Balfour in imperial developments through his entire career was best reviewed in a London dissertation and book by Denis Judd [207, 208]. Such factors as Joseph Chamberlain's machinations as Colonial Secretary, the free trade-tariff reform debate, the status of India, the Union of South Africa, and pressure from Ireland to alter the oath to the British Crown were all pertinent. Balfour was directly identified with many of these issues. He had already initiated the strategic defense structure of the empire, the Committee of Imperial Defence.

The Balfour Report of 1926, sometimes called the Balfour Definition, articulated the basis for the Statute of Westminster of 1931, the constitution of the British Commonwealth of Nations. At the Imperial Conference of 1926, Balfour, because of his prestige as former Prime Minister and senior statesman, chaired a special committee to draft a definition of the Commonweath. The Report, which took Balfour's name, was entitled "Report of the Inter-Imperial Relations Committee of the Imperial Conference of 1926." Two works by K.C. Wheare [407, 408], W.D. McIntyre [244], Nicholas Mansergh [251], and, in German, Hans Bartschi [40] described these developments. Preliminaries were the subject of a Harvard dissertation and book, both by Aaron Friedberg [140, 141].

DIPLOMACY

Arthur James Balfour entered politics as Member of Parliament in 1874. He accompanied his uncle, then Foreign Secretary Lord Salisbury, to the international Congress of Berlin of 1878. While Balfour was deputy to Prime Minister Lord Salisbury and, then, as Prime Minister, British strategic and foreign policy was reoriented, from "splendid isolation" to alliances and ententes, first with Japan, later with France and Russia. This was all part of the system of alliances preliminary to the outbreak of World War I. During the war, Balfour served as First Lord of the Admiralty, in the small War Cabinet under

David Lloyd George, and as Foreign Secretary in that coalition government during and after the war.

The best overview of these British foreign policy matters was a three volume survey by C.J. Lowe [236]. William N. Medlicott [261] wrote the most detailed account of the Congress of Berlin of 1878. Balfour attended as the private secretary to his uncle, the Foreign Secretary in the Disraeli government. Later, when Balfour was Prime Minister, one of the most disruptive crises with which Balfour had to contend was a direct confrontation between Lord Curzon, Viceroy of India, and Field Marshal Kitchener, commander of British forces in India. Both were powerful and opinionated figures. A London dissertation by John Lydgate [238] discussed this imbroglio. Curzon eventually resigned and left India.

Throughout his political career, most of the late nineteenth century, Lord Salisbury was most identified with foreign policy. Even though he served as Prime Minister, his monument is located in the Foreign Office in Whitehall. A substantial book by John Grenville [171] and a pamphlet by Lilian Penson presented an overview of his foreign policy achievements. Most significant of those achievements was the major reorientation of British imperial and foreign policy at the end of the century. Great Britain had prided itself through the nineteenth century with its aloof policy of "splendid isolation," powerful enough to remain above European and international conflicts. The international situation changed toward the end of the century. The Boer War became a quagmire for British forces. Isolation appeared increasingly dangerous. France, Russia, and Germany were expanding, Japan was flexing her muscles, and even the United States was gaining colonial possessions and expanding her armed forces. Salisbury was credited with reorienting British imperial and international policies from splendid isolation to creation of a system of alliances prior to World War I. These matters were reviewed by Michael Hurst [192], in an Indiana dissertation by Israel Tarkow-Naamani [371], and in a Cambridge dissertation and book by George Monger [268, 269].

John A. White [409] has just published a book, Transition to Global Rivalry: Alliance Diplomacy and the Quadruple Entente. This described the diplomatic restructuring at the turn of the century. The "quadruple" meant Great Britain, Japan, France, and Russia, previously competitors and potential enemies, all of whom perceived the rising threat of Germany and its allies, Austria, for a moment, Italy, and the Ottoman Empire as serious enough to combine international and military interests.

The first step for Great Britain was to negotiate an alliance with Japan; the subtitle of the best account, by Ian Nish [286], was The Diplomacy of Two Island Empires. Nish [285] wrote a follow-up account of the later disposition of the alliance. The noted diplomatic historian, Zara Steiner [368], wrote an article analyzing the making of the alliance.

Far more significant in the reorientation of British imperial and foreign policies at the turn of the century was the negotiation of ententes, first with France and then with Russia, signed in 1904 and 1907, respectively. For these, most of the work was accomplished during the Balfour administration. Here, the best diplomatic histories were by Samuel Williamson [417] and a book and article by Keith Wilson [418, 419]. In the impressive Making of the Twentieth Century series, Zara Steiner [367] presented the comprehensive summary of the origins of the war from the British perspective. The individual contribution and role of Balfour in all of this was presented in a recent Oxford dissertation and book by Jason Tomes [385, 386]. A general survey of these decades before the war was by Barbara Tuchman [389], The Proud Tower, a popular history approach.

In the Lees Knowles Lectures at Cambridge of 1957, John Ehrman [118] reviewed Cabinet government in wartime in the first half of the twentieth century. He credited the initiatives of Balfour in founding the Committee of Imperial Defence and his continued participation and support. Balfour gave credit to Lord Hankey as the organizer of the war effort. Michael Dockrill [101] and John Turner [390] have both edited surveys of British policy during the war. Turner [391], in another recent study, focused on the process of coalition Cabinets and the war. The Liberal Prime Minister H.H. Asquith first ran the war with his Party government. Balfour had been brought in to participate on the Committee of Imperial Defence before the war began. In May 1915, there was a crisis and Asquith formed the first coalition government. Balfour served as First Lord of the Admiralty. Lloyd George took the powerful position as Minister of Munitions. An essay on the making of the first coalition was by Peter Fraser [133].

In December 1916, a second government crisis came to a head. Asquith must go was a common feeling, so must Balfour from the Admiralty. A few even wanted Balfour to become Prime Minister. David Lloyd George won out and became Prime Minister of a war coalition government; Balfour was made Foreign Secretary. Robert Scally [337] and David French [139] have conducted extensive studies of the Lloyd George coaliton. An Oxford dissertation by I.A. Rose [323] focused on the Conservative Party and the Lloyd George coalition. Lloyd George was the subject of biographies by A.J. P. Taylor [375] and Bently Gilbert [150]. Gilbert's biography was two volumes, the second volume entitled The Architect of Victory. A new analysis of British foreign policy during the early 1920s was by G.H. Bennett [47].

Other personalities associated with foreign policies require introduction. The British Foreign Office always had influential and powerful civil servants. Two during the Balfour era were Baron Hardinge of Penhurst, the biography by Briton Busch [71], and Sir Eyre Crowe, the biography by Sibyl Crowe [91]. Curzon was Viceroy of India; another Viceroy who served on the War Cabinet during the war was Viscount Milner, noted as a strategist of the war. The study was by N.T.A. Forster [129]. Lord George Curzon, the former Viceroy, actually succeeded Balfour as Foreign Secretary. To begin with, there was a new bibliography by James Parker [294] in Greenwood's Bibliographies of British Statesmen series. There was a recent biography by David Gilmour [154], over 700 pages, and older ones by Kenneth Rose [325], almost 500 pages, and Sir Harold Nicolson [282]. The next Foreign Secretary, from 1924 to 1929, was Austen Chamberlain, heir to Joseph and older brother to Neville Chamberlain. Chamberlain [76] wrote a memoir. A biography was by David Dutton [109] and a recent Oxford dissertation on Chamberlain was by R.S. Grayson [167].

Balfour became Foreign Secretary in December 1916, the Armistice was signed in November 1918, the Peace Conference which met at the Versailles Palace just outside Paris lasted from January to June 1919. Balfour was technically responsible. However, Lloyd George liked to work more with personal advisers, his so-called "Garden Suburb." Nevertheless, the Foreign Office carried out massive studies of past peacemaking, precedents of the past, territorial boundaries, and other research, all in preparation. Ultimately, the map of Europe and much of the world was redrawn. Balfour was one of the members of the Council of Ten which made most of the decisions. Then Balfour often represented Great Britain at the newly formed League of Nations. Balfour actually chaired the Peace Conference on occasion. Later, Balfour directly oversaw the financial arrangements for the treaty with Austria.

The extensive process of preparation, formulating British war aims, and peace planning was described by V.H. Rothwell [329] and Erik Goldstein [156]. The standard history of the Peace Conference, 6 volumes, was by Harold Temperley [377]. Other accounts were by E.J. Dillon [99], Harold Nicolson [284], and F.S. Marston [256]. The recent authoritative study, in The Making of the Twentieth Century series, was by Alan Sharp [352]. Participants assessed the process: Lord Hankey [180] and John Maynard Keynes [217]. Keynes, Treasury Office representative, became disenchanted, opposed the punitive measures against Germany, and wrote a scathing critique of the conference. The diplomatic historian, Michael Dockrill [100], wrote an analysis.

The typical big power delegation to the Versailles Peace Conference consisted of the head of state and foreign minister; Balfour seconded Prime Minister David Lloyd George for the British Delegation, both being members of the Council of Ten. On occasion, Balfour sat in the British seat and on occasion, chaired deliberations, first for the Peace Conference, and later for the League of Nations.

Balfour concentrated on the issue of Austria and the Austrian war debts. He oversaw the ultimately successful process of saving Austrian financial institutions and the government of Austria. Balfour [18] himself wrote an outline of possible boundary adjustments for Europe which was published. A critique of the Austrian financial provision, including the reparations problem, was by Manfred Bansleben [39], in German. The author praised the sensible proposals of Keynes but they were rejected; Balfour's plan, more punitive, was adopted.

The term "special relationship" has been used by scholars and analysts to describe Anglo-American relations. Balfour was a contributor to the phenomenon at several points in his career as international statesman.

Early in 1917, the role of the United States in World War I was becoming an increasingly crucial issue. The Germans announced resumption of unrestricted submarine warfare to commence 1 February 1917. President Woodrow Wilson objected. Soon there was the inevitable incident involving deaths of Americans.

Under these circumstances, Wilson invited an official delegation to the United States to discuss coordination of war planning. Balfour was to chair the delegation. The group travelled by sea, Greenock, Scotland to Halifax, Nova Scotia on OLYMPIC and by train to Washington, arriving 22 April and staying for four weeks. Balfour met with Wilson and addressed the U.S. Congress. The final chapter, Chapter 17, of his autobiography [17], which otherwise ended with the 1880s, described this official visit.

As a former Prime Minister and senior statesman, Balfour led an official visit to the United States in the spring of 1917. He addressed the U.S. Congress and negotiated with President Woodrow Wilson. He met leaders of the Jewish community and gained their support, and eventually that of Wilson, for the Balfour Declaration. Late in 1921, Balfour returned as head of the British delegation to the Washington Conference on disarmament and Pacific area rectifications. At an interview with American reporters, Balfour [25] spoke on freedom of the seas, published in pamphlet form.

About the time the British delegation was in the United States in the spring of 1917, the U.S. declared war against Germany. Balfour played a role. In a new book on the American presidency and secret intelligence operations, Christopher Andrew [9] of Cambridge University recounted the following series of events: British intelligence operatives in "Room 40," the famous intelligence center during World War I, decrypted the Zimmermann Telegram, an offer by Germany to Mexico to enter the war as an ally. There was more than one source. One was opening of the German diplomatic pouch which went through London, something that would have been universally condemned, if made public. The Foreign Office was reluctant to inform the United States. It was Balfour who decided to personally pass the information to the American Ambassador, contending access from a different source (p. 43). That was in February 1917. The United States declared war on Germany in April.

In another recent review of Anglo-American relations at this time, David Woodward [422] of Marshall University noted that Balfour gave Wilson copies of the secret treaties concluded by the Allies before and during World War I. This occurred during the Balfour mission. U.S. officials, including Wilson and Congress, were impressed with the dignity, tactfulness, and intelligence of Balfour (pp. 50-67). Other writing on Anglo-American relations during this crucial time were a book and an article by Kathleen Burk [68, 69] and a book by G.R. Conyne [87]. Burk stressed that Great Britain was increasingly dependent on financial support by the United States.

Three and a half years later Balfour was back. This time he was official head of the British delegation to the Washington Conference which opened on 12 November 1921 and concluded on 6 February 1922. There were several pressing matters which President Herbert Hoover and others hoped to resolve. The first was arms limitation, especially naval warship limitation. The disposition of China and the threat to the Open Door Policy, a favorite issue of the United States, and defense matters related to the Pacific Ocean area were two other issues. The Americans and British hoped to avoid the potential costs of a naval arms race. The participants were the U.S., Great Britain, Japan, France, Italy, China, Belgium, Holland, and Portugal. A series of treaties were signed: recognition of the integrity of China, agreements on future defense measures for the Pacific Ocean area, and a 5:5:3 tonnage ratio of capital ship fleets for the U.S., Great Britain, and Japan, respectively.

The Washington Conference has been touted as a major event in arms limitation. Richard Burns [70] edited a comprehensive bibliography on that topic for the ABC-Clio War/Peace Bibliography series, with 8847 entries. It was also a favorite topic for Ph.D. dissertations: Phillips O'Brien [289] for Cambridge University, D.J. Shorney [354] for Durham University, R.W. Anderson [8] for the University of Kentucky, and Raymond Gamble [144] for the University of Massachusetts. Both O'Brien and Anderson noted that Great Britain ceded its historic claim to naval superiority.

The latest and best study of the Washington Conference was by Erik Goldstein [156], a series of ten essays by experts with a foreword by Ernest R. May. Certain observations and conclusions were informative. Financial pressures and Anglo-American anxiety about Japan were important. In the naval arms agreement the focus was on battleships and battle cruisers, no agreements being reached on aircraft carriers and submarines nor on the future place of Germany as a naval power. The conclusion was that it failed and there were serious consequences; the subtitle ended with the phrase . . . the Road to Pearl Harbor. The essay by Goldstein described the process of acquiring the members of the British delegation (pp. 21-28). Responsibility was placed on CID, upsetting the Foreign Office. Balfour was absent in Geneva chairing a session of the League of Nations, so he was selected to head the delegation. Balfour was not pleased and suggested Bonar Law. Lloyd George considered going and Winston Churchill supported that. The delegation departed on 16 October 1921, still no decision had been reached. Balfour finally received the appointment by default.   The delegation was praised for the largest number of objectives achieved. Other works on the Washington Conference were by Thomas Buckley [67] and Robert Van Meter [264].

Chapter 9

Assessments and Areas for Future Research

ASSESSMENTS

Arthur James Balfour has been commemorated in art, sculpture, and literature. Three portraits can be found, at the Carlton Club, at Trinity College, Cambridge, and at Eton School. There was a bust at Whittingehame.

The most notable statue was the official one at Parliament unveiled on 9 May 1962 by then Prime Minister Harold Macmillan. It was by David McFall [243], seven feet tall, in French limestone, and located in the Members' Lobby outside the House of Commons. McFall was paid ten thousand pounds. Next to Balfour is Henry Asquith in marble. Lloyd George and Winston Churchill are in more expensive bronze. An earlier model had Balfour with a golfing cap but it was rejected by the authorities.

Balfour was the subject or model in fictional works. Anthony Trollope [387] wrote an unfinished novel, The Landleaguers, in the 1880s in which Irish uprisings were depicted. He was employed as a postal clerk in Ireland and boycotts and land uprisings occurred in his district. Balfour and repression figured in the plot.

H.G. Wells [403, 404], the famous author and futurist, met Balfour at Stanway House in Gloucestershire. Balfour later appeared in two of the novels of Wells, as Evesham in The New Machiavelli and as Cecil Burleigh in Men Like Gods. Characteristics of both were clearly identifiable with those of Balfour. The autobiography of H.G. Wells [402] referred to the Balfour-Chamberlain debate over tariff reform and the Souls. From John Buchan [66], Lodge in the Wilderness, Balfour, and also, apparently, Lord Rosebery, an earlier Liberal Prime Minister, were the models of the imperialist character, Lord Appin.

Balfour was a favorite subject for cartoons. An example was by Francis Brown [65], The Doings of Arthur, a timely satirical survey of his premiership published in 1905. Observations about intellectual pursuits, Ireland, education reform, "Hotel Cecil," and his views about newspapers were all satirized. A general survey of cartoons and the Prime Minister was by Kenneth Baker [15]. Balfour (pp. 130-39) was depicted by Max Beerbohm as "a wilting question mark" and by Punch as steering Salisbury away from obstacles. Ian McDonald [241] wrote an article on postcards and politics which included depictions of Balfour in cartoon form, for example, satirizing him as an opponent of protection.

In July 1928, on the occasion of his 80th birthday, both Houses of Parliament presented Balfour, the great elder statesman, with a new Rolls Royce automobile.

AREAS FOR FUTURE RESEARCH

None of the several biographies of Arthur James Balfour, by Dugdale [104], Mackay [245] Egremont [116], Young [423], and Zebel [424], were satisfactory. Only Mackay was up to date but there were gaps in the coverage and research. Some were limited by the fifty-year rule which no longer applies. Dugdale was constrained by family factors and was dated. Egremont was a politician. Young was a journalist. Zebel, an academic scholar, was limited by rules for a biographical series and it was comparatively short.

So there is need for a solid, scholarly, comprehensive, i.e., political, personal, and intellectual, biography which incorporates all of the variety of aspects of the life of Balfour and all of the latest interpretations and sources. It should be substantial. Balfour was involved in so many different things and each needs to be fully pursued and elaborated upon. Then, all must be properly integrated, balanced, and placed in perspective. Serious consideration should be given to producing an official, three-volume, Victorian-type biography. The official biography of Winston S. Churchill was eight volumes plus dozens of supplemental volumes, written by Martin Gilbert [152]. Surely Balfour deserves three volumes for his modern official biography.

Care should be taken in the new, comprehensive biography to fill gaps. The factors of Balfour as philosopher and Balfour as psychic have never been sufficiently or appropriately integrated into the literature about Balfour. The "authorized" biography, by the niece, Blanche Dugdale, as an afterthought, added an unsatisfactory appendix by an academic, explaining the philosophy of Balfour. Most biographies and related studies completely ignore the psychic phase. Spiritualism, Theosophy, and Psychic Research were prominent movements and closely related during the late nineteenth and early twentieth centuries in Great Britain and the United States. Balfour was President of the Society for Psychic Research and participated in seances. Obviously that aspect of his life and the movement should be considered and integrated into pertinent surveys and assessments.

Obviously, from the chapter on the Balfour Declaration, a vast literature has accumulated on that subject. Equally important was the process of gaining approval of the concept and the aquisition of the Mandate for Palestine for Great Britain. The Zionists were just as active at the Paris Peace Conference and the Arabs presented their opposition. This was a neglected aspect and needs development and elaboration. Indeed, more needs to be written about these matters from the Arab perspective.

Finally, one other gap potentially can be filled. Balfour was ahead of his time as a motor car enthusiast. Similarly, he was an early supporter and active observer of innovations in aviation. He personally attended early demonstrations and perceived the capabilities of this new dimension. This aspect needs further study and development. That important contribution of Balfour should be highlighted.

Part II
Annotated Bibliography

1   Abdy, Jane. The Souls. London: Sidgwick, 1984, 192 pp. About the extraordinary group prominent in society in the late nineteenth century, Balfour, "King Arthur," seen as the most important member; introduction followed by individual chapters on members, e.g., Lord Curzon, Balfour (pp. 30-45), the Duchess of Rutland, Lady Desborough, and St. John Broderick, and couples, e.g., the Custs, Windsors, Elchos, and the Tennant family.

2   Abels, Jules. The Parnell Tragedy: The Story of a Great Man and a Fatal Flaw. NY: Macmillan, 1966, 408 pp. An undistinguished account of the rise and fall of Charles Stewart Parnell, the Irish leader of the 1880s and 1890s; a prominent antagonist of Balfour.

3   Adelson, Roger. London and the Invention of the Middle East: Money, Power, and War, 1902-1922. New Haven: Yale UP, 1994, 1995, 256 pp. The issue of the Middle East defined the political agenda; involved the government, the banks, and the military strategists; most important personalities were Balfour, Churchill, Lloyd George, and Curzon; at the time London was the international center of capitalism, finance, trade, communications, and media; the Balfour Declaration was a decisive factor; not a Jewish conspiracy, not humanitarian, not hasty, but deliberate and calculated and dependent upon American approval.

4   -------. Mark Sykes: Portrait of an Amateur. London: Cape, 1975, 336 pp. Sykes was the British official instrumental in the making of the Balfour Declaration.

5   Adonis, Andrew. Making Aristocracy Work: The Peerage and the Political System in Britain, 1884-1914. Oxford Historical Monographs. Oxford: Clarendon, 1993, 324 pp. A demonstration of revival of interest in the aristocracy, especially the House of Lords; revived an older thesis that the aristocracy of Great Britain was not declining but adapted and revived, exerting powerful influence; Salisbury, Landsdown, and Balfour were outstanding examples, but Balfour was less able to stem the tide of declining power.

6   Alderson, Bernard. Arthur James Balfour: The Man and His Work. London: Richards, 1903, 379 pp. One of the earliest biographies of Balfour, upon the occasion of his becoming Prime Minister; seen as a "Statesman, Legislator, Leader, Politician, and Colleague, and in his private life as an Author and Landowner"; recalled Balfour in the Fourth Party and as Irish minister.

7   Allen Peter. The Cambridge Apostles: The Early Years. Cambridge: UP, 1978, 276 pp. An elite intellectual club founded at Cambridge University in 1820; membership was secret; among the series of notable members was Balfour while he was at Cambridge.

8   Anderson, Russell W. "The Abandonment of British Naval Supremacy, 1918-1920." Ph.D. diss, Kentucky, 1974, 193 pp. A dissertation under J.A. Thompson; the issue was maintenance of British naval superiority; American insistence on freedom of the seas was diverted but American naval parity had to be accommodated.

9   Andrew, Christopher. For the President's Eyes Only: Secret Intelligence and the American Presidency from Washington to Bush. NY: HarperCollins, 1995, 672 pp. A series of case studies of codebreaking and intelligence incidents; pertinent to Balfour, the case of the Zimmermann Telegram, January 1917, when the British intercepted the German secret offer inviting Mexico to join in alliance; British intelligence officials feared exposure of methods but Balfour, as Foreign Secretary, intervened, personally presenting a copy to the American Ambassador; President Wilson was shocked and America soon entered the war.

10   Anstey, Joanna and Silverlight, John, eds. The "Observer" Observed, 1791-1991: 200 Years of Distinguished Writing from One of the World's Great Newspapers. London: Barrie, 1991, 304 pp. Northcliffe and Astor were owners in the first decades of the twentieth century; J.L. Garvin was editor and he was recipient of much official information from Fisher and Balfour, among others.

11   Arnstein, Walter L. The Bradlaugh Case: A Study in Late Victorian Opinion and Politics. Alt. subtitle: Atheism, Sex and Politics among the Late Victorians. London: Oxford UP; Columbia: UP Missouri, 1965, 1984, 387 pp. The standard account of this sensational political case during the 1880s in the House of Commons; Charles Bradlaugh, an avowed atheist, was elected for Northampton but was voted not to be seated, reelected, not seated, reelected, and finally seated; Gladstone backed seating and Conservatives obstructed the process, Balfour being a leader in obstruction.

12   "Arthur James Balfour, first Earl of Balfour, 1848-1930." Dictionary of National Biography, 1922-1930. London: Oxford UP, 1937, pp. 41-56. Essay by Algernon Cecil; Balfour was a "philosopher and statesman" (listed in that order); noted his mediocre performance at Eton and Cambridge; his philosophy was closest to that of the eighteenth century; he always controlled his emotions, seemingly was insincere; founder of "the Souls"; his tenure as minister for Ireland was a "personal triumph"; tenure as Prime Minister featured establishment of CID and debate over free trade; later became a great statesman; Zionism and the Balfour Declaration; role in the peace conference and Washington Conference; other achievements.

13   Ayerst, David. Garvin of the "Observer". London: Helm, 1985, 326 pp. Garvin was editor, 1908-1942; a Unionist newspaper and Garvin enjoyed extraordinary access to powerful government officials, e.g., Balfour and Fisher.

14   Bagehot, Walter. The English Constitution. World's Classics series. Introduction by Earl of Balfour. London: Oxford UP, 1928, 340 pp. Originally published in 1867; the introduction was signed by Balfour at Whittingehame, November 1927; he noted Bagehot had described how Great Britain was governed; most of foreign examples he cited were American; Balfour explained differences between British and American governments.

15   Baker, Kenneth. The Prime Ministers: An Irreverent Political History in Cartoons. London: Thames, 1995, 192 pp. Over 200 illustrations of cartoons about Walpole and those who followed up to Thatcher and Major; including Max Beerhohm cartoon, "Balfour and the Policeman" of 1911; others on Balfour, pp. 130-41.

16   Balfour, Arthur James. Catalogue of Old English Silver Plate, the Property of the Late Rt. Hon. the Earl of Balfour . . . also Part of the Scarsdale Heirlooms . . . Auction July 16, 1930. London: Clowes, 1930, 19 pp. The illustrated catalogue for Christie's auction sale of some properties of Balfour, conducted within a few months after his death.

17   -------. Chapters of Autobiography. Alt. title: Retrospect: An Unfinished Autobiography, 1848-1886. London: Cassell; NY: Houghton, 1930, 256 pp. Edited by Blanche E.C. Dugdale; Balfour began writing his memoirs early in 1928, never finished; chapters on childhood, school at Eton and Cambridge, tennis, friends, music, adventures on Skye, philosophy, recollections

of Disraeli and Gladstone, the Fourth Party, "the Souls," and a trip to America in 1917; most coverage up to the time he became Chief Secretary for Ireland; described himself as "a very lazy man who has always had a job on hand."

18 -------. [Confidential Memoranda on Possible Boundary Re-adjustments in Europe]. London: Foreign Office, 1918. Signed "A.J.B."; an outline of a proposal for national boundaries for Europe after the First World War; the map of Europe was eventually redrawn.

19 -------. A Defence of Philosophic Doubt. London: Macmillan, 1879, 1920. An edition of 1000 copies paid for by Balfour; eventually a success and reissued in 1920; speculation about the tensions between religious and scientific beliefs; Oscar Wilde called it "one of the dullest books we know."

20 -------. The Education Bill 1902: Speech in the House of Commons. London: Eyre, 1902, 36 pp. Balfour was the most prominent proponent of the Education Act passed in 1902.

21 -------. Financial Relations between Great Britain and Ireland . . . . A Speech in the House of Commons on the 5th of July 1898. London: Conservative, 1898, 24 pp. In the previous two decades, Balfour was a most prominent spokesperson for the government on Ireland.

22 -------. Fiscal Reform: Speeches Delivered from June 1880 to December 1905. . . . London: Conservative, 1906. A series of speeches by Balfour on financial issues; included correspondence with Joseph Chamberlain on the issue of free trade.

23 -------. The Foundations of Belief: Being Notes Introductory to the Study of Theology. London: Longman, 1895, 1896, 1901, 1906, 435 pp. The most important treatise by Balfour on philosophy, going through at least 8 editions (with a new introduction by Balfour in 1901) and translations into French, German, and Italian.

24 -------. A Fragment on Progress: Inaugural Address Delivered on His Installation as Lord Rector of the University of Glasgow, November 1891. Edinburgh: Douglas, 1892, 73 pp. Balfour was an elected official to a number of universities, this one, Glasgow in 1891.

25 ------. The Freedom of the Seas: Interview Given by the Rt. Hon. A.J. Balfour (To the American Press). London: Unwin, 1916, 11 pp. Statements by the First Lord of the Admiralty about a topic which is highly sensitive in Anglo-American relations.

26   -------. Handel. Reprint from The Edinburgh Review. London, 1887, 56 pp. Balfour was a prominent patron of classical music and his favorite composer was Handel.

27   -------. "Review of Morley's Life of Cobden." Nineteenth Century, 11 (n.d.): 40-55. A book review in a prominent periodical.

28   -------. Opinions and Arguments from Speeches and Addresses, 1910-1927. NY and London: Hodder, 1927, 1928, 323 pp. Selections made by Blanche Dugdale, Balfour's official biographer; a wide variety of addresses; included some correspondence with his literary agent.

29   -------. Passages in His Non-Political Speeches, Addresses and Writings. London: Longman, 1913, 234 pp. Edited by J.G. Jennings and abridged from W.M. Short; a series of addresses of a non-political nature.

30   -------. Some Economic Notes on Insular Trade. London: Longman, 1903. Balfour articulated his thoughts on free trade, an issue of much significance; outlined his fiscal policy; recommended "retaliation, tariff by tariff"; noted fear of split in the Unionist Party over this issue; especially controversial was taxes on food.

31   -------. Speeches on Zionism. London: Arrowsmith, 1928, 128 pp. By this time Balfour was an international celebrity associated with Zionism, especially revered by Jews.

32   -------. Theism and Humanism: Being the Gifford Lectures, 1914. London: Hodder; NY: Doran, 1915, 289 pp. The first series of Gifford Lectures, University of Glasgow; ten lectures in this series, also translated into French and Italian.

33   -------. Theism and Thought: Second Course of Gifford Lectures, 1922-1923. London: Hodder, 1923, 293 pp. Continuation of the Gifford Lectures by Balfour.

34   Balfour Papers. Various and various locations: originally held in the Tower, Whittinghame estate (the Tower has been refurbished and is the current home of the present Earl of Balfour, great nephew of the first Earl), subsequently moved to the Scottish Record Office, Edinburgh; details about Whittingehame can be found at the National Register of Archives, Edinburgh (copies at the Institute of Historical Research and Scottish Universities); an extensive collection, 280 bound volumes, is held in the Balfour Papers, Add. Mss # 49683-49962, at the British Library; an extensive collection of official papers are housed in the PRO, Kew; others at the University Library, Cambridge University and the Perkins Library, Duke University, Durham, NC.

35   Balfour of Whittingehame. <u>Muniments-Handlist</u>. Scottish Record Office.   Order numbers GD433/2, 3529 items held since February 1987; examples included details about Whittingehame and the other Balfour estate at Strathconan, 1817-1929; ledgers, cash books, and farm records.

36   Balfour. <u>Whittingehame and Strathconan Papers Handlist</u>. Reference # GD 433/1.   Estate volumes, 1817-1922.   Legal and estate papers of Balfour properties in Scotland; items formerly held in the Tower at Whittingehame until 1963; included miscellaneous papers on topics such as Zionism, naval reforms, correspondence with W.T. Stead about political prospects, and CID.

37   Balfour. "Visit with Earl Balfour, 1 June 1994." An interview of the Third Earl Balfour by Eugene Rasor at the Tower, Whittingehame. Discussion about the disposition of Whittingehame House: the estate is in trust; in the 1930s, a home for Jewish refugee children who were allowed to leave Germany, then a home for Scottish orphan children to 1952, later converted into seven apartments by Alan Cope, the owner in 1994; the Balfour and Traprain titles went to a nephew in 1930; the current holder is a grand nephew and he has no direct heir; it is anticipated that the title will be contested in court.

38   Ball, Stuart. "The Conservative Party and British Politics, 1902-1940." <u>Historian</u>, 33 (Winter 1991): 9-11. Most historians have focused on the rise of Labor and decline of Liberals; the Conservatives have been neglected; the dominating personalities in the first decade of the century were Balfour and Joseph Chamberlain.

39   Bansleben, Manfred. <u>Das Osterreichische Reparationsproblem auf der Pariser Friedenskonferenz</u>. Vienna: Bohlau, 1988, 171 pp.   The financial arrangements between Austria, a successor state from the defunct German Empire, and the Allies were negotiated by Balfour; Austria was to pay reparations.

40   Bartschi, Hans E. <u>Die entwicklung vom imperialischen Reichsgedanken zur modernen Idee des Commonwealth in Lebenswerk Lord Balfour</u>. Aarau,

1957. A German account about Balfour and the formulation of the concept of the British Commonwealth.

41 Bates, Jean V. Sir Edward Carson: Ulster Leader. Introduction by A.J. Balfour. London: Murray, 1921, 76 pp. A work about Carson and the problems in Northern Ireland; Balfour noted Carson was an old friend and credited him with "saving Ulster."

42 Baylen, Joseph O. [A Biography of W.T. Stead]. Forthcoming. Professor Baylen has written several articles on W.T. Stead, the influential editor of The Pall Mall Gazette, and is preparing a new biography.

43 Beardslee, C.G. "Arthur James Balfour's Contribution to Philosophy." Ph.D. diss, Brown, 1931. An older dissertation about Balfour and his philosophy.

44 Beaverbrook, Baron Max Aitken. Men and Power, 1917-1918. London: Collins, 1956, 1966, 448 pp. By an influential newspaper owner-politician; a series of mini-biographies, e.g., Balfour, pp. ix-xxvi, who was "much admired . . . . and it is just possible that he didn't believe in anything or anybody"; Asquith described him as a man of "superficial charm."

45 -------. Politicians and the War, 1914-1916. 2 vols. NY: Doubleday; London: Butterworth, 1928, 1960, 1967, 613 pp. Related to the previous entry; an inside assessment of politics and the war.

46 Beckett, Ian F.W. and Gooch, John, eds. Politicians and Defence: Studies in the Formulation of British Defence Policy, 1845-1970. Manchester: UP, 1981, 224 pp. Eight essays by prominent historians on noted reformers at the War Office, e.g., Cardwell, Arnold-Forster, Haldane, and Kitchener; Balfour credited with facilitating reforms in the Army.

47 Bennett, G.H. British Foreign Policy during the Curzon Period, 1919-1924. NY: St. Martin, 1995, 254 pp. Curzon was Foreign Secretary after Balfour, a very complicated time for British foreign policy; a world war had concluded and several empires had disappeared, e.g., the German, Austrian, Russian, and Ottoman; also a time when Lloyd George increasingly depended on personal, non-governmental advisers; a comprehensive overview.

48 Bentwich, Norman. Fulfilment in the Promised Land, 1917-1937. London: Soncino, 1938, 256 pp. About the Balfour Declaration and its consequences, cultural, economic, agricultural, and social; the attempt at a bi-national state eventually failed.

49   Blake, Lord Robert. The Conservative Party from Peel to Thatcher. Alt. subtitle: From Peel to Churchill. London: Fontana, 1970, 1985, 402 pp. The Ford Lectures at Oxford, 1968 by a distinguished political historian; the Conservative Party is the longest-lived political party and its evolution has been "jerky and discontinuous" with frequent adaptations; pertinent chapter, "Defeat and Recovery, 1902-1922," pp. 167-200; when Salisbury resigned in 1902 Joseph Chamberlain was the best known possible successor but an injury and the past actions of Chamberlain meant the choice was Balfour; Balfour credited with successes in foreign policy, defence, education, and Ireland but there were blind spots, e.g., labor unions and the debate over tariff reform; Balfour deserved blame for the "insane decision" (p. 190) to reject the Budget of 1909.

50   -------. and Cecil, Hugh, eds. Salisbury: The Man and His Policies. London: Macmillan, 1987, 307 pp. A series of essays on the uncle-Prime Minister and mentor of Balfour.

51   Blewett, Neal.   "Free Fooders, Balfourites, Whole Hoggers: Factionalism within the Unionist Party." Historical Journal, 11 (1968): 95-124. The unity of the Unionist party ended with the speech of 15 May 1903 in Birmingham by Joseph Chamberlain on free trade; conpared it to the nailing of the 95 Theses by Martin Luther; focused on the consequences, election defeats of 1906 and 1910; the 3 fragmented successors: Unionist free traders, Chamberlainite tariff reformers, and Balfourite fence-sitters.

52   -------. The Peers, the Parties and the People: The British General Election of 1910. London: Macmillan; Toronto: UP, 1972, 548 pp. A political assessment of the two elections of 1910; serious constitutional issues were at stake, the role of the House of Lords.

53   Blumenthal, Harvey. "W.T. Stead's Role in Shaping Official Policy: The Naval Campaign of 1884." Ph.D. diss, George Washington, 1984, 306 pp. A dissertation under Robert Kenny; an outstanding case study of the influence and power of Stead who was fed official information by Jacky Fisher; Balfour later maintained close contact with Stead.

54   Blunt, W.S. My Diaries: Being a Personal Narrative of Events, 1888-1914. London: Seeker; NY: Knopf, 1919, 1923, 1932, 930 pp. Many references to Balfour related to this activist in the Irish question, at one time jailed when Balfour was Chief Secretary.

55   Bonham Carter, Violet. <u>Lantern Slides: The Diaries and Letters of Violet Bonham Carter, 1904-1914</u>. London: Weidenfeld, 1996, 491 pp. Ed. by Mark Bonham Carter and Mark Pottle; introduction by Roy Jenkins; by the only daughter of the Prime Minister, H.H. Asquith, and a close friend of Balfour whom she said was "the most all-around perfect being I've ever met"; also a friend of the Elchos.

56   -------. "The Souls." <u>Listener</u>, October 1947. A short article on the intellectual clique founded by Balfour.

57   Boyce, D. George, ed. <u>The Crisis of British Unionism: Lord Selborne's Domestic Political Papers, 1885-1922</u>. London: Historians, 1987, 286 pp.   This compilation focused on domestic political matters; a Liberal Unionist who was related to Balfour and the Salisburys; he called the Parliament Bill of 1911, "Emasculation of the House of Lords and Establishment of the House of Commons as a single chamber Tyranny" Bill (p. x).

58   -------. <u>The Irish Question and British Politics, 1868-1996</u>. <u>British History in Perspective</u> series. NY: St. Martin's, 1996, 192 pp.   About the "oldest question" and attempts to formulate a solution; coverage of most recent events.

59   -------. <u>Nineteenth-Century Ireland: The Search for Stability</u>. NY: Barnes, 1990, 354 pp. A recent history of the Irish Question during the long nineteenth century, 1798-1923; Balfour was most involved in the 1880s and 1890s.

60   Bralley, H. "St. Loe Strachey and the Politics of Dilemma: A Study of Political Journalism during the Edwardian Era." Ph.D. diss, South Carolina, 1971. A dissertation about journalists and political influence early in the century.

61   Brendon, Piers. <u>Eminent Edwardians</u>. London: Deutsch, 1979, 1981, 1996, 269 pp. Extended profiles of 4 Edwardians: Northcliffe, Mrs. Pankhurst, General Baden-Powell, and Balfour (pp. 65-130); in the tradition of <u>Eminent Victorians</u> by Lytton Strachey, presenting pithy and penetrating analyses of representative figures; Balfour was "enigmatic," the last hereditary ruler of the Tory party; "flirted with spiritualism"; an "anti-Semitic Zionist"; included a long list of nicknames.

62   Briggs, Asa, ed. <u>Longman Dictionary of Twentieth-Century Biography</u>. London: Longman, 1985, 558 pp. Entry on Balfour (p. 31), "British statesman and Conservative prime minister. . . ."; mention of Ireland, Balfour Declaration, Education Act, and CID; last phrase: "also a philosopher."

63   Brock, Michael and Brock, Eleanor, eds. <u>H.H. Asquith: Letters to Venetia Stanley</u>. NY: Oxford UP, 1982, 696 pp. An incredible series of 560 letters (about half are included) from the Prime Minister to a young woman in her 20s, Venetia Stanley, who later married Edwin Montagu; Balfour is mentioned several times: Asquith respected him, Margot suspected him; topics included secrets related to the army, navy, Ulster, and prominent political personalities; the dates are 1909-1915 and the Prime Minister was in the midst of war preparation and war--he describes all to her.

64   Brooks, David. <u>The Age of Upheaval: Edwardian Politics, 1899-1914</u>. <u>New Frontiers in History</u> series. Manchester: UP, 1995, 224 pp. Described the Edwardian era as a "formative period of unprecedented assertiveness and aggression" (blurb); chapter on "the Unionist Debacle, 1902-1905" (pp. 42-89); Balfour hoped to avoid a showdown within the Unionist party; 1903 was the worst year, the year of resignations of Chamberlain and others; Balfour was determined to cling to power, meantime he "squandered a substantial political inheritance" (p. 4).

65   Brown, Francis. <u>The Doings of Arthur</u>. London: Methuen, 1905, 51 pp. A small folio size by a caricaturist; "Being a Trifling account of the Amazing Adventures of Arthur during the past three years" (p. 1); why the job: "belong to the Only Family! Being a bachelor-he knows what's best for kids"; "Arthur's Amusements: writes books and things, he don't read newspapers, plays at goff"; "all Arthur's good men left except the Dook-then the Dook left, then Arthur brings in a lot of dummy's in place of the men what was gone"; and more satirical journalistic musings.

66   Buchan, John. <u>A Lodge in the Wilderness</u>. London: Nelson, 1906, 1917, 1922, 378 pp. A novel about imperialism by the prolific fiction writer, e.g., <u>39 Steps</u>; Lord Appin was modeled on a mixture of Lord Rosebery and Balfour.

67   Buckley, Thomas H. <u>The United States and the Washington Conference, 1921-1922</u>. Knoxville: UTennP, 1970, 236 pp. An account from the American perspective of the arms limitation conference; Balfour led the British delegation.

68   Burk, Kathleen M. <u>Britain, America and the Sinews of War, 1914-1918</u>. Boston and London: Allen, 1984, 1985, 296 pp. Focused on the economic and financial relationships between the U.S. and Great Britain during the war; Great Britain was close to bankruptcy, America shifted from neutrality to anti-German stance, financed the Allied war effort, and superseded Great Britain as the hegemonic power; several British missions to arrange financing and repayment arrangements, some headed by Balfour.

69   -------. "The Diplomacy of Finance: British Financial Missions to the U.S.A." Historical Journal, 22 (June 1979): 351-72. Great Britain became increasingly dependent on American finance; a series of missions to the U.S.; Balfour headed an important one on 1917; over the next two years Britain borrowed 4 billion dollars; Great Britain now humiliatingly dependent on the U.S.; Great Britain permanently lost international financial hegemony.

70   Burns, Richard Dean, comp. Arms Control and Disarmament: A Bibliography. War/Peace Bibliography series. Oxford: ABC-Clio, 1977, 446 pp. An extensive bibliography, 8847 entries, on arms control and disarmament.

71   Busch, Briton C. Hardinge of Penhurst: A Study of the Old Diplomacy. Conference on British Studies Biographies series. Hamden: Archon, 1980, 381 pp. An enlightening account of Hardinge, permanent undersecretary at the Foreign Office when Balfour was Foreign Secretary; Hardinge considered Balfour "not up to the daily grind" (p. 256), thus increasing the work and responsibility of Hardinge; other critical assessments of Lloyd George, Lord Esher, and Mark Sykes, all influential in policy; e.g., Sykes, who arranged the Balfour Declaration was an amateur, a "most dangerous" person.

72   Butler, Larry and Gorst, Anthony, eds. Modern British History: A Guide to Study and Research. NY: St. Martin's; London: Tauris, 1997, 288 pp. A recent survey of the process and status of research on twentieth-century British history.

73   Campbell, N.J.M. Jutland: An Analysis of the Fighting. London: Conway; Annapolis: NIP, 1986, 447 pp. The most detailed and most thorough study of the battle, its tactics, weaponry, who fired what and when, and the damage and damage control, ship by ship on both sides; from the British point of view, Jutland was "a thoroughly unsatisfactory battle" (p. 337) but the German fleet was in no position to fight at the end; British and German gunnery was about even and the percentage of hits was about the same.

74   Cecil, Lady Gwendolen G. Biographical Studies of the Life and Political Character of Robert, Third Marquis of Salisbury. London: Hodder, 1948, 96 pp. A short biographical study of Salisbury.

75   -------. Life of Robert, Marquis of Salisbury: By His Daughter. 4 vols. London: Hodder, 1921-1932. A lengthy biography of Salisbury by the daughter who was knowledgeable and served as his private secretary; never fully completed.

76   Chamberlain, Sir Austen. Politics from Inside: An Epistolary Chronicle, 1906-1914. New Haven: Yale UP, 1937, 676 pp. By the son of Joseph Chamberlain; much on the tariff reform issue, Joseph's "sacred cause"; critical observations of many prominent British officials.

77   The Chamberlain Papers: From the University of Birmingham Library. Woodbridge: Primary Source, n.d., microfilm. Ed. by Peter T. Marsh; 61,000 items on microfilm of the papers of Joseph, Austin, and Neville Chamberlain, father and two sons; much detail on Joseph Chamberlain.

78   Charmley, John. A History of Conservative Politics in Britain, 1900-1996: The Quest for Power. NY: St. Martin's; London: Macmillan, 1996, 290 pp. A history of the party from Salisbury to John Major by a noted revisionist historian; one of 12 chapters, "Balfourian Dog Days."

79   Churchill, Winston S. "Arthur James Balfour." Strand, April 1931. A short recollection of Balfour by his friend and colleague, Churchill.

80   -------. Lord Randolph Churchill. 2 vols. NY: Macmillan, 1906, 1951, 926 pp. Winston Churchill prepared and wrote this major biography of his father partly to vindicate and rehibilitate him and his reputation; Lord Randolph Churchill rose rapidly in politics, formulated the concept of Tory Democracy, and fell from grace just as rapidly.

81   -------. The World Crisis. 6 vols. NY: Scribners, 1923-1931, 1951, 1963, 2700 pp.; other editions: 4 vols., 1950, 1964; 2 vols., 1939; 1 vol., 1951, 1960, 1996, 866 pp. Churchill's history of the First World War and its aftermath; the expected eloquence and brilliant observations plus the personal experience; Balfour at the Admiralty and Jutland in Vol. III; Churchill a partisan for Admiral Beatty and critical of Admiral Jellicoe; Balfour read and assessed: "Winston's brilliant autobiography, disguised as a history of the universe" (Egremont, Balfour, p. 321).

82   Clarke, Peter. Hope and Glory: Britain, 1900-1990. Penguin History of Britain # 9. London: Lane, 1996, 480 pp. A new survey of the twentieth century, replacing the old Pelican History series; emphasis on political history; refused to describe Great Britain as "in decline."

83   -------. A Question of Leadership: Gladstone to Thatcher. London: Hamilton, 1991, 344 pp. An idiosyncratic assessment; 10 Prime Ministers and 4 leaders; Balfour not featured; Gladstone was the most important in the nineteenth century; Joseph Chamberlain was the first modern politician; noted the lost causes of Winston Churchill: gold, India, and Edward VIII.

84   Coetzee, Frans. For Party or Country: Nationalism and the Dilemmas of Popular Conservatism in Edwardian England. NY: Oxford UP, 1990, 231 pp. A proliferation of political pressure groups characterized the period and most were Conservative: e.g., Navy League, National Service League, and the Tariff Reform League, the one with which Balfour had to contend more than any other; the culmination was the Diehards who caused emasculation of the House of Lords.

85   Coles, Alan. Slaughter at Sea: The Truth Behind a Naval War Crime. London: Hale, 1986, 220 pp. A shrill indictment of the Royal Navy for perpetrating the HMS BARALONG incident: a British Q-Ship flying the American flag, 19 August 1915, surprised and sank U-27, murdering crew survivors; Coles claimed the Admiralty was to blame, covered up the incident, that the war was prolonged leading to the rise of Hitler; concluded the British were just as evil as the Germans; Balfour was First Lord at this time.

86   Conservative Party Archive. Bodleian Library, Oxford University, Oxford, England. The papers, documents, and records of the Conservative Party of Great Britain were deposited at this famous library of Oxford University. The archive is also available on microfilm; an important source; Balfour was leader of the Party, 1902-1911, and an important participant before and after that.

87   Conyne, G.R. Woodrow Wilson: British Perspectives, 1912-1921. London: Macmillan, 1992, 256 pp. The impact of Wilsonian diplomacy on Anglo-American relations; Wilson dealt most closely with Lloyd George and Balfour; he was an Anglophile but was critical of "the old diplomacy"; Britain, France, and Italy were upset with his meddling; enlightening on how Anglo-American relations changed because of Wilson.

88   Cook, Chris, et al., comps. The Longman Guide to Sources in Contemporary British History. 2 vols. London: Longman, 1994, 700 pp. A reference guide to assist historical research; on organizations, pressure groups, and individuals, e.g., the Zionists.

89   ------- and Waller, David, comps. Sources in British Political History, 1900-1951. 7 vols. London: Macmillan; NY: St. Martin's, 1975-1993, 1500 pp. A standard reference guide, extensive and frequently updated on all types of sources on 20th-century political British history.

90   Craton, Michael and McCready, H.W. The Great Liberal Revival, 1903-1906. London: Hansard, 1966, 47 pp. A short survey of a decisive period in the history of the Liberal Party; Balfour and his government held on to power longer in hopes that old divisions within the Liberal Party would prevent the formation of a viable government; Campbell-Bannerman succeeded in holding the party together and winning a landslide election victory in 1906.

91   Crowe, Sibyl and Corp, Edward. Our Ablest Civil Servant: Sir Eyre Crowe, 1864-1925. London: Merlin, 1993, 550 pp. A new biography of the influential head of the Foreign Office, notably during the series of crises leading to the First World War and during the peace conference; credited with the massive process of preparation for the conference and advising Lloyd George and Balfour in Paris.

92   Cruise O'Brien, Conor. Parnell and His Party, 1880-1890. Oxford: Clarendon, 1957, 373 pp. A thorough examination of Parnell, more on the party; Balfour involved.

93   Curtis, Lewis Perry. Anglo-Saxons and Celts: A Study of Anti-Irish Prejudice in Victorian England. Studies in British History and Culture. NY: NYUP, 1968, 162 pp. Curtis has written extensively and persuasively on anti-Irish prejudice during the time Balfour was Chief Secretary; this Victorian racism was fatal to Home Rule and demonstrated how a myth can determine national policy.

94   -------. Apes and Angels: The Irishman in Victorian Caricature. Washington: Smithsonian, 1971, 1996, 208 pp. New introduction and two new chapters in 1996 edition; a continuation of the expose of anti-Irish prejudice, this focusing on Victorian cartoons, e.g., about "Paddy" and Darwin's "missing link."

95   -------. Coercion and Conciliation in Ireland, 1880-1892: a Study in Conservative Unionism. Princeton: UP, 1963, 460 pp. Curtis saw Balfour as the Chief Secretary who combined the two elements of Irish rule, coercion and conciliation, for the specific purpose of killing Home Rule once and for all (p. viii); Wilfrid Blunt accused the Balfour brothers of "scientific inhumanity" in Ireland (p. 177).

96   -------. "The Salisbury Administration and Ireland, 1885-1892." D.Phil. diss, Oxford, 1959. A dissertation which became the basis for the previous entries.

97   Dangerfield, George. The Strange Death of Liberal England, 1910-1914. NY: Capicorn, 1935, 1961, 449 pp. A classic and fascinating analysis of the end of the Liberal Party as a viable entity; the Dangerfield thesis, highly controversial, stressed the problems created by the women's and labor movements and Ireland; instrumental was the crisis over the House of Lords.

98   Davis, Richard W. The English Rothschilds. London: Collins; Chapel Hill: UNCP, 1983, 272 pp. The Jewish family of Rothschilds were wealthy and powerful in Europe and in Great Britain; the Balfour Declaration was in fact a letter to Lord Rothschild, the noted spokesperson for Jews in Great Britain.

99   Dillon, E.J. The Inside Story of the Peace Conference. NY: Harper, 1920, 513 pp. A contemporaneous account of the Versailles peace conference.

100   Dockrill, Michael L. and Goold, J.D. Peace without Promise: Britain and the Peace Conference, 1919-1923. London: Batsford, 1981, 287 pp. A thorough survey of British policies at the Versialles Peace Conference, e.g., case studies of Belgium, Italy, Austria, and the Balfour Declaration.

101   ------- and French, David, eds. Strategy and Intelligence: British Policy during the First World War. London: Hambledon, 1996, 229 pp. A series of essays with up-to-date appraisals of British policies during the war.

102   D'Ombrain, Nicholas J. "Churchill at the Admiralty and the Committee of Imperial Defence, 1911-1914." JRUSI, 115 (March 1970): 38-41. Much is made of a crucial meeting of CID at the time of the Agadir crisis when it was clear the navy was unprepared for war; Churchill was brought in as First Lord to create a naval staff and prepare for war; Balfour had remained active on CID.

103   Drexel, John, ed. The Facts on File Encyclopedia of the Twentieth Century. NY: Facts on File, 1991, 1058 pp. Included a mini-biography of Balfour, pp. 68-69; a review of his political career, e.g., education reform in 1902 and the Anglo-French entente in 1904; the Balfour Declaration was his most important achievement.

104   Dugdale, Blanche E.C. Arthur James Balfour, First Earl Balfour. 2 vols. London: Hutchinson, 1936, 1937, 898 pp. The official biography of

Balfour by his devoted niece; credited Professors Pringle Pattison and L.B. Namier for assistance; examples of coverage: Jutland and the Admiralty communique, the Balfour mission to America in 1917, the making of the Balfour Declaration, and the Balfour Report of 1926; the blurb claimed access to all Balfour papers and that Balfour was "the most distinguished, the most discussed and least understood statesman of modern times," plus more hyperbole.

105   -------. Baffy: The Diaries of Blanche Dugdale, 1936-1947. London: Vallentine, 1973, 262 pp.   Ed. by N.A. Rose; the niece and biographer of Balfour; contributed to perpetuating Balfour's association with Zionism.

106   -------. The Balfour Declaration: Origins and Background. London: Jewish Agency, 1940, 32 pp. A portrait of Balfour and a copy of the declaration were included; the occasion was the 10th anniversary of the death of Balfour; critical of the British government for just having limited immigration of Jews into Palestine, seen as sacrificing "Jewish national rights on the altar of Arab desires" (p. 5).

107   -------.   Family Homespun.   London: Murray, 1940, 205 pp. Reminiscences of Mrs. Dugdale; recollections of "Uncle Arthur" at Whittingehame, e.g., body guards on the grounds when he was Chief Secretary for Ireland, the presence of The Souls and their party games on weekends in September, and Balfour's first automobile.

108   -------. Dugdale Papers. In possession of Michael Dugdale. The papers collected by Blanche Dugdale for the biography of Balfour.

109   Dutton, David J. Austen Chamberlain: Gentleman in Politics. Bolton: Anderson, 1985, 383 pp.   The son of Joseph Chamberlain, "Joe's standard bearer," and later foreign minister after Balfour.

110   -------. "His Majesty's Loyal Opposition": The Unionist Party in Opposition, 1905-1915. Liverpool Historical Studies # 11. Liverpool: UP, 1992, 331 pp. Balfour and Bonar Law led this opposition and the issues were constitutional reform, tariff reform, social reform, and Ireland; the defeat of 1906 was a disaster and the party was neither united nor had a coherent programme.

111   -------. "Life Beyond the Political Grave: Joseph Chamberlain, 1906-1914." History Today, 34 (May 1984): 23-28. Chamberlain had resigned his offices to campaign for tariff reform and he remained a powerful political force until his actual death.

112 -------. "Unionist Politics and the Aftermath of the General Election of 1906." Historical Journal, 22 (December 1979): 861-76. A review of the causes of the electoral disaster of 1906 and interpretations about who was in charge: Balfour, Joseph Chamberlain, or others; the Conservatives would be unable to form a government on their own until 1922.

113 Eaglesham, Eric. From School Board to Local Authority. London: Routledge, 1956, 230 pp. Re the Education Act of 1902; Balfour perceived the importance of reform in the administration of education and proceeded to lead a successful effort, resulting in the connection of local administration with local finance; the old school boards were abolished.

114 -------. "Planning the Education Bill of 1902." British Journal of Educational Studies, 9 (November 1960): 3-24. Balfour was one of three who were most instrumental in educational reform; credited as "the founder of a national system of education" (p. 23).

115 Eccleshall, Robert. English Conservatism since the Reformation: An Introduction and Anthology. London: Unwin, 1990, 264 pp. An idiosyncratic assessment of the history of the Conservative party, including Edmund Burke, Peel, Disraeli, Joseph Chamberlain, Balfour of Burleigh, etc., but Balfour is barely mentioned.

116 Egremont, Max. Balfour: A Life of Arthur James Balfour. London: Collins, 1980, 391 pp. A relatively recent and readable biography; access to Whittingehame papers; claims new material, fresh sources, and emphasis on political and personal aspects; Balfour was one of the wealthiest young men in Great Britain but over the years lost it all due to careless management; his objective as a philosopher was to reconcile religion and science; Hankey credited Balfour with creation of CID; reviewed Balfour's relations with Chaim Weizman; at the time of the government crisis of December 1916, Lord Robert Cecil and Milner were for Balfour as Prime Minister; informative on the last years, illness, and death.

117 -------. The Cousins: The Friendships, Opinions and Associations of Wilfrid Scawen Blunt and George Wyndham. London: Collins, 1977, 320 pp. Blunt and Wyndham were cousins and close friends and Balfour appeared frequently in their lives, especially when Ireland was involved; Balfour and Wyndham had gone to school together, the latter being the protege; Blunt was pro-Irish and was actually imprisoned over the question.

118   Ehrman, John. <u>Cabinet Government and War, 1890-1940</u>. Cambridge: UP; NY: Archon, 1958, 1969, 138 pp.   The Lee Knowles Lectures at Cambridge, 1957; the process of the conduct of war and government; Balfour launched CID based on the War Council and Army and Navy Committee and attended the meetings; noted the famous meeting of 23 April 1911 exposing the unpreparedness of the navy; Balfour credited Hankey with the effectiveness of CID.

119   Ellenberger, Nancy W. "The Souls and London Society at the End of the Nineteenth Century." <u>Victorian Studies</u>, 25 (Winter 1982): 133-60. The Souls consisted of about 40 friends and relatives, especially from 5 families including Balfour, in London society in the decades before World War I, the most famous social coterie of the time; noted for intellectualism and esoteric conversation.

120   Englefield, Dermot, et al. <u>Facts about the British Prime Ministers: A Compilation of Biographical and Historical Information</u>. London: Mansell, 1995, 473 pp. Foreword by John Major; from Walpole to Major including Balfour (pp. 217-22); a chronological survey with much detail, e.g., constituencies: Hertford, Manchester-East, and the City of London.

121   Ensor, R.C.K. <u>England, 1870-1914</u>. <u>Oxford History of England</u>. London: Oxford UP, 1936, 1949, 1986, 1992, 634 pp. A classic history of the period; covered the time Balfour entered politics, rising to Prime Minister.

122   Epstein, Klaus W.   <u>The British Constitutional Crisis, 1909-1911</u>. <u>Garland Outstanding Dissertations</u> series. NY: Garland, 1987, 1989, 544 pp. Foreword by Stephen Graubard; this British dissertation by a noted historian of Germany; featured the political conflict between Campbell-Bannerman and Balfour, described as "the most striking figure in English politics" (p. 8); the conflict began with the Budget of 1909 and culminated with the Parliament Act of 1911.

123   Esher, Viscount Oliver, ed. <u>The Captains and Kings Depart: Journal and Letters of Reginald Viscount Esher</u>. 4 vols. NY: Scribners, 1934-1938. Esher, 1852-1930, was the "Colonel House" of Kings Edward VII and George V, i.e., very influential; purposely avoided publicity.

124   Evans, Brendan and Taylor, Andrew.   <u>From Salisbury to Major: Continuity and Change in Conservative Politics</u>. NY: St. Martin's; Manchester: UP, 1996, 300 pp. The Conservative party was able to maintain itself in power by adapting; noted a break in 1965 when the first non-aristocrat became leader and characterized by Thatcherism.

125   Fair, John and Hutcheson, John A.   "British Conservatism in the Twentieth Century: An Emerging Ideological Tradition." Albion, 19 (Winter 1987): 549-78. The rise of socialism and labor forced the Conservative party to define its ideology and image; Joseph Chamberlain and Lord Hugh Cecil, son of Salisbury, are singled out, representing articulation of the ideology during the Balfour era.

126   Fanning, J.R. "Arthur Balfour and the Leadership of the Unionist Party in Opposition, 1906-1911: A Study of the Origins of the Unionist Policy towards the Third Home Rule Bill."   Ph.D. diss, Cambridge, 1968.   A dissertation which stressed the role of Balfour and the Irish problem, this time while leader of the Opposition; the Third Home Rule bill was passed but abandoned when the First World War began.

127   Farr, Barbara S. The Development and Impact of Right-Wing Politics in Britain, 1903-1932.   NY: Garland, 1987, 133 pp.   A study of the development of the Right, the origins being from tariff reformers and imperialists; during the Balfour era, factors were the budget battle, the Parliament Act, and opposition to socialism; ultimately there were fascist tendencies.

128   Fletcher, Sheila. Victorian Girls: Lord Lyttelton's Daughters. London: Hambledon, 1997, 288 pp. The Lyttelton family included members of the Souls and others close to Balfour, especially the daughter, May, daughter of the 4th Lord Lyttelton, to whom Balfour was almost engaged at the time of her death; Lucy married Lord Frederick Cavendish, murdered in Phoenix Park, Dublin, in the late 1880s.

129   Forster, N.T.A.   "The Religio Milneriana and the Lloyd George Coalition, 1916-1921." Ph.D. diss, Keele, 1980. Re the ministerial career of Lord Milner, one of the 5-man War Cabinet, Balfour being another; emphasis on the military policies of the war.

130   Foster, Janet and Sheppard, Julia, eds. British Archives: A Guide to Archive Resources in the United Kingdom. NY: Stockton, 1982, 1984, 1989, 1991, 1995, 892 pp. Over 1200 entries of locations of archives and research associations, e.g., Record Offices, libraries, and museums.

131   Foster, Robert F. <u>Lord Randolph Churchill: A Political Life</u>. Oxford: Clarendon, 1981, 440 pp. An undistinguished biography of the leader of the Fourth Party and prominent Unionist leader.

132   Francis, Martin and Zweiniger-Bargielowska, Ina, eds.   <u>The Conservatives and British Society, 1880-1990</u>. Cardiff: UWalesP, 1996, 342 pp. A collection of essays about aspects of conservatism: national identity, ideology, the love-hate relationship with the British public, and gender.

133   Fraser, Peter. "British War Policy and the Crisis of Liberalism in May 1915." JModHis, 54 (March 1982): 1-26. A series of incidents, e.g., Fisher resigning as First Sea Lord and the "shell-shortage" scandal, forced Asquith to form a coalition; that meant the end of Liberalism.

134   -------. <u>Joseph Chamberlain: Radicalism and Empire, 1868-1914</u>. London: Cassell, 1966, 349 pp. A political biography of the great statesman; blended radicalism and imperialism.

135   -------. "Lord Beaverbrook's Fabrications in <u>Politicians and the War, 1914-1916</u>." HJ, 25 (March 1982)Z: 147-66. Beaverbrook claimed his account of the fall of Asquith and creation of a coalition government was correct; in fact, it was full of fabrication and "amateurish conjectures of an outsider" (p. 150), but, curiously, it has remained influential.

136   -------. <u>Lord Esher: A Political Biography</u>. London: Hart, 1973, 508 pp. A biography of the influential, behind-the-scenes official with access to the Crown; associated with CID.

137   -------. "Unionism and Tariff Reform: The Crisis of 1906." HJ, 5 (1962): 149-66. Leading up to the election, a defeat for the Unionists, party infighting involving Joseph Chamberlain and the issue of tariff reform increased; the test was loyalty to Balfour but his position was ambigious.

138   -------. "The Unionist Debacle of 1911 and Balfour's Retirement." JMODHIS, 35 (September 1963): 354-65. On 8 November 1911, Balfour announced retirement from the leadership position, satisfying the "Balfour Must Go!" contingent; objections were political and personal; he had tried to remain aloof but "forward leadership" was needed; the Conservative party of 1911 was no longer amenable to personal authority but was not yet ready for the machine politician.

139   French, David. The Strategy of the Lloyd George Coalition, 1916-1918. Oxford: Clarendon, 1995, 344 pp. A new comprehensive study of the making of war strategy by the coalition government of Lloyd George; the debate between the "brass hats" (generals) and the "frock coats" (politicians); the objective was to win the war, and, perhaps more importantly, win the peace; e.g., the mission of Balfour to the U.S. in 1917.

140   Friedberg, Aaron L. "Change Assessment and Adaptation: Britain and the Experience of Relative Decline, 1895-1905." Ph.D. diss, Harvard, 1986, 556 pp. A dissertation under Stanley Hoffman on the perceptions of British leaders during the Balfour era; indicators in commerce, seapower, and national power created concern.

141   -------. The Weary Titan: Britain and the Experience of Relative Decline, 1895-1905. Princeton: UP, 1988, 345 pp. Based on the dissertation, about the alarm of British statesmen over decline, economically, navally, militarily, and morally; an assessemnt of the official mind, a construct of Paul Kennedy.

142   Friedman, Isaiah. The Question of Palestine, 1914-1918: British-Jewish-Arab Relations. London: Routledge; NY: Transactions, 1973, 1992, 498 pp. A thorough examination of the issues leading to the Balfour Declaration, covered in chapter 18 (pp. 309-32); an important British concern was propaganda and outbidding the Germans in attracting support from Jews; disagreed that Balfour Declaration was due to miscalculation.

143   Fromkin, David. Peace to End All Peace: Creating the Modern Middle East, 1914-1922. London: Deutsch; NY: Holt, 1989, 1990, 635 pp. The title was from Archibald Wavell, a veteran of the Allenby campaign, describing the Versailles Settlement; noted the power of the Jewish vote in Britain, e.g., in Manchester, the constituency of Balfour and Churchill.

144   Gamble, Raymond C. "Decline of the DREADNOUGHT: Britain and the Washington Naval Conference, 1921-1922." Ph.D. diss, Massachusetts, 1993, 440 pp. A dissertation on naval aspects of the Washington Conference; Balfour headed the British delegation.

145   Garvin, J.L. and Amery, Julian. The Life of Joseph Chamberlain. 6 vols. London: Macmillan, 1932-1969, 3300 pp. The standard biography and a model for Victorian multi-volume biography; the first 3 volumes were by the noted journalist, J.L. Garvin, and the last 3 volumes by Julian Amery, not completed until 1969; focused on politics and speeches; little on the economic implications of tariff reform.

146   Garvin, J.L. Papers of J.L. Garvin. University of Texas, Austin. The papers of Garvin, one of the most important of a group of journalists early in the century with contacts and influence among prominent politicians, e.g., Balfour, Fisher, Esher, and Lloyd George; held at the University of Texas Library.

147   Gelber, Nathan Michael. Hatzharath Balfour Vetoldoteha [The Balfour Declaration and Its History]. In Hebrew. An account of the making of the Balfour Declaration; based on the description by Herbert Samuel.

148   Gibbs, Norman H. The Origins of Imperial Defence: An Inaugural Lecture Delivered before the University of Oxford on 8 June 1955. Oxford: Clarendon, 1955, 24 pp. A description of the formation of CID; an analysis of the background: originally defense of the British Isles was the concern during the age of sail; steam power and imperial expansion meant new and different problems; to defend the empire; and the disasters of the Boer War convinced all of the need for planning and preparation.

149   Gibson, R.S. "Balfour and Education, 1896-1911." Ph.D. diss, Liverpool, 1992. Re the involvement of Balfour in the reform, improvement, and expansion of education; he emphasized the role of the established church and Parliament; concluded that Balfour was strongly committed to education as the highest priority, even above tariff reform.

150   Gilbert, Bentley B. David Lloyd George: A Political Life. 2 vols. Columbus: Ohio State UP, 1987-1992, 1070 pp. The first of two of a projected multi-volume political biography; covered up to 1916 and Balfour figured prominently throughout; Gilbert has a low opinion of other biographies.

151   Gilbert, Martin. Jerusalem in the Twentieth Century. London: Chatto, 1996, 400 pp. By the prolific official biographer of Churchill and other histories about Jews; for the 3000th anniversary of the holy city; coverage of the impact and consequences of the Balfour Declaration which politicized everything; no leading nation has recognized Jerusalem as capital.

152   ------- and Churchill, Ranfolph. Winston S. Churchill. 8 vols. Boston: Houghton; London: Heinemann, 1961-1989, 8856 pp. The massive official biography of Churchill begun by his son, Randolph, and completed by Gilbert; more supporting volumes to come: 14 companion volumes published; much detail on day-to-day activities and little interpretation; assessed as too detailed and boring; noted that Balfour asked Churchill to draft a second, more inspiring Jutland communique (vol. III, p. 777); later, in the 3rd volume of The World Crisis, Churchill jumped into the Jutland controversy with 62 pages of critique.

153   Gillon, D.Z.   "The Antecedents of the Balfour Declaration."   Middle Eastern Studies, 5 (May 1969): 131-50. About the British debate over Palestine and the motivations; but these were not influential on the government; the "ardent Zionism" of Balfour was after the fact; Balfour had almost nothing to do with the declaration (pp. 140-143).

154   Gilmour, David.   Curzon.   London: Murray, 1994, 684 pp.   A biography of one of the great viceroys and foreign secretaries; successor to Balfour in the latter position; created a controversy during 1905 in a conflict in India over civilian control of the military, a fight with Kitchener which Curzon lost and resigned.

155   Glubb, John B.   Britain and the Arabs: A Study of Fifty Years, 1908 to 1958. London: Hodder, 1959, 496 pp. Focused on Anglo-Arab relations and the rise of Arab nationalism; obviously the Balfour Declaration was covered (pp. 72-75, 131-42); claimed no rational explanation for the reasons the declaration was issued; many Jews opposed Zionism and even the Zionists were surprised; Lloyd George seemed to have exerted the most influence.

156   Goldstein, Erik D. and Mawer, John, eds.   The Washington Conference, 1921-1922: Naval Rivalry, East Asian Stability and the Road to Pearl Harbor. Portland, OR: Cass, 1993, 1994, 327 pp. Foreword by Ernest R. May; 10 essays on various aspects of the Washington Conference which averted a naval arms race and avoided conflict in the Pacific; forthcoming on the choice of Balfour to head the British delegation (pp. 21-28); Balfour was in Geneva and the CID (with Balfour absent) called for a "political heavyweight"; Balfour was not pleased and suggested others; Lloyd George considered going and Churchill supported that; ultimately the choice was a good one and Britain emerged with most aims achieved.

157   -------.   Winning the Peace: British Diplomatic Strategy, Peace Planning, and the Paris Peace Conference, 1916-1920. NY: Oxford, 1991, 326 pp. The Foreign Office Political Intelligence Department played the most important role in the planning, led by Lord Hardinge, Arnold J. Toynbee, and John Maynard Keynes; over 200 reports were prepared; some disputes between the Foreign Office and Lloyd George's "Garden Suburb"; Balfour deferred to Lloyd George; Balfour was depicted as "ever the conciliator and postponer" (p. 177).

158   Gollin, Alfred M. Balfour's Burden: Arthur Balfour and Imperial Preference. London: Blond, 1965, 303 pp. The "burden" is Joseph Chamberlain and the tariff reform and imperial preference campaign; Chamberlain saw these matters as solving what he and his supporters saw as increasing threats to the British Empire; "one of the fiercest controversies in modern British political history" (p. 32); Balfour attempted a truce and personally conducted an extensive study assisted by experts, all the while appearing as lazy, bored, and indifferent; his primary goal was to remain in office to complete key measures such as CID, the Anglo-Japanese Alliance, and military reforms.

159   -------. The Impact of Air Power on the British People and Their Government, 1909-1914. Studies in Military and Strategic History. London: Macmillan, 1989, 366 pp. Balfour played a role in the expansion of air power by participation in discussions and displays of planes of the Wright Brothers and with encouragement of scientific advances; as Opposition leader, he endorsed the plans of the Liberal government.

160   -------. "The Observer" and J.L. Garvin, 1908-1914: A Study in a Great Editorship. London: Oxford UP, 1960, 445 pp. Garvin repeatedly gained special access to government and official information and support, e.g., with Fisher when the navy was internally divided, the Fisher-Beresford conflict; Fisher also fed Garvin information assisting in articles about the rising German naval threat.

161   Gooch, John. "The Chiefs of Staff and the Higher Organization for Defence in Britain, 1904-1984." NWCR, 49 (January 1986): 53-65. From lessons of the Boer War, military staff and war planning was adopted, somewhat haphazardly; by 1904 there was a permanent secretariat and Balfour supported the process.

162   -------. The Plans of War: The General Staff and British Military Strategy, 1900-1916. London: Routledge; NY: Wiley, 1974, 362 pp. The CID performed these functions after 1902 but the navy was not always cooperative; Lord Esher was instrumental in the strategic shift from an imperial to a continental strategy; Balfour had pushed for an imperial defense organization beginning in the 1890s.

163   -------. "Sir George Clark's Career at the CID, 1904-1907." HJ, 18 (September 1975): 555-69. Clark was secretary of CID, the first "defence bureaucrat"; Balfour and Esher instrumental in the development.

164 Goodman, Paul, ed. The Jewish National Home: The Second November 1917-1942. London: Dent, 1943, 320 pp. Foreword by Viscount Cecil of Chelwood; a commemoration of the 25th anniversary of the Balfour Declaration sponsored by the Zionist Federation; important to stress that it was a Cabinet decision; Balfour saw it as his most important action.

165 Goring, Rosemary, ed. Chambers Scottish Biographical Dictionary. Edinburgh: Chambers, 1992, 508 pp. The Balfours (pp. 23-25); accounts of the first Earl, George Balfour, founder of Balfour Beatty Ltd., the second Earl, Gerald William Balfour, 1853-1945, brother of AJB.

166 Gorst, Harold E. The Fourth Party. London: Smith, 1906, 334 pp. Preface by Sir John Gorst; a history of the group, Lord Randolph Churchill, Balfour, Sir Henry Drummond Wolff, and John Gorst; active, 1880-1885, "a brilliant and meteoric career, . . . practically unparalleled in politics" (p. 1); Balfour was seen as "the odd man"; first surfaced during the imbroglio over Charles Bradlaugh and the Parliamentary oath.

167 Grayson, R.S. "Austen Chamberlain and British Foreign Policy, 1924-1929." D.Phil. diss, Oxford, 1995. A dissertation on Chamberlain, successor to Balfour at the Foreign Office; Balfour stood in for him on occasion.

168 Green, E.H.H., ed. An Age of Transition: British Politics, 1880-1914. Edinburgh: UP, 1997, 130 pp. A new survey of this crucial period for the Conservative party.

169 -------. The Crisis of Conservatism: The Politics, Economics and Ideology of the British Conservative Party, 1880-1914. London: Routledge, 1995, 1996, 426 pp. The Conservative party has been in power longer than any party in Europe, yet there is one period preferably forgotten, the first two decades of the 20th century; included election defeats of 1906 and two in 1910; the slide began in 1903 with Chamberlain and the tariff reform campaign; yet the 20th century became the Conservative century.

170 -------. "The Strange Death of Tory England." 20th Century Britain, 2 (1991): 67-88. A review of 6 works; the Conservatives have been in power 67 of the past 100 years; the pre-1914 fratricidal struggle was debilitating, leading to 3 defeats.

171 Grenville, John A.S. Lord Salisbury and Foreign Policy at the Close of the Nineteenth Century. University of London Historical Studies # 14. NY: Oxford UP, 1964, 1970, 451 pp. Re the readjustment of British foreign policy,

1895-1902; issues were the Boer War, the Anglo-Japanese Alliance, Fashoda, and the China question.

172   Grieb, Conrad K. The Balfour Declaration: Warrant for Genocide. NY: Examiner, 1972, 122 pp. A critical study with an exaggerated subtitle.

173   Griffiths, Dennis. The Encyclopedia of the British Press, 1422-1992. NY: St. Martin's, 1992, 702 pp. A history of British journalism; during the late 19th and early 20th centuries a skillful use of the press was demonstrated by such politicians as Joseph Chamberlain, Rosebery, Balfour, and especially Lloyd George; noted editors were W.T. Stead, J.A. Spender, C.P. Scott, and J.L. Garvin.

174   Hale, Oron J. The Great Illusion, 1900-1914. The Rise of Modern Europe series # 18. NY: Harper, 1971, 361 pp. A volume in a classic series on European history; placed the Balfour era in a larger context.

175   -------. Publicity and Diplomacy: With Special Reference to England and Germany, 1890-1914. NY: Appleton; Gloucester, MA: Smith, 1940, 1964, 486 pp. Thesis: the mass circulation press was a dynamic force in Great Britain and Germany with malevolent consequences; contributing to the deterioration of Anglo-German relations.

176   Hammond, J.L. C.P. Scott of the "Manchester Guardian. London: Bell, 1934, 379 pp. Charles Prescott Scott, 1846-1932, editor of the Manchester Guardian, very influential, especially in the matter of advocacy for Zionism and contacts between Balfour and Weizmann.

177   Hanham, H.J., ed. Bibliography of British History, 1851-1914. Oxford: UP, 1976, 1633 pp. For the American Historical Association and the Royal Historical Society; c. 11,000 entries of books and articles published up to 1972.

178   -------. "The Creation of the Scottish Office, 1881-1887." Juridical Review, 1965, pp. 205-44. An account of the office; Balfour was Chief Secretary.

179   Hankey, Maurice P.A. The Supreme Command, 1914-1918. 2 vols. London: Allen; NY: Macmillan, 1961, 932 pp. By Lord Hankey, secretary of CID, 1908-1938, based on his diaries; close adviser to Balfour and others; credited the organizational genius of Lloyd George with winning the war.

180   -------. The Supreme Control at the Paris Peace Conference, 1919: A Commentary. London: Allen, 1963, 206 pp. A sequel to the previous entry; an overview of the peace conference; informative on the prominent personalities including Balfour.

181   Hardie, Frank and Herrman, Irwin. Britain and Zion: The Fateful Entanglement. Belfast: Blackstaff, 1980, 128 pp. A short explanation of the relationship.

182   -------. "The King and the Constitutional Crisis of 1911." History Today, 20 (May 1970): 338-47. A history of the rise of Parliament, division into two houses, priority for finance bills in the House of Commons, and the unprecedented nature of the Lords rejecting the budget of 1909; precipitated the constitutional crisis which was prolonged by the death of Edward VII; resolved by the Parliament Act of 1911; Balfour figured prominently in this.

183   Harris, Jose and Hazlehurst, Cameron. "Campbell-Bannerman as Prime Minister." History, 55 (October 1970): 360-83. Re the successor to Balfour; informative on the meeting in Scotland in the fall of 1903 which resulted in a successful plan to form a unified cabinet ready to take office after the election of 1906; few believed Campbell-Bannerman could do it.

184   Harris, Paul. Life in a Scottish Country House: The Story of A.J. Balfour and Whittingehame House. Whittingehame: Whittingehame, 1989, 144 pp. Access to Balfour papers in describing the house, an architecturally important building and the home of a political family; advertised for sale in 1986: 60 rooms, 33 bedrooms, estimated value: 120,000 pounds.

185   Havighurst, Alfred F. Britain in Transition: The Twentieth Century. Alt. title: Twentieth-Century Britain. NY: Harper; Chicago: UP, 1979, 667 pp. A substantial historical survey of the 20th century with several editions.

186   -------. Modern England, 1901-1970. Alt. title: 1901-1984. NY: Cambridge UP, 1976, 1987, 119 pp. For the Conference on British Studies; a short text-survey of the 20th century.

187   Hazlehurst, Cameron. "Asquith as Prime Minister, 1908-1916." ENGHISREV, 85 (July 1970): 502-31. A political history of the Asquith regime concluding: "It was a melancholy end" (p. 530) due to lack of initiative and executive incompetence.

188   ------- and Woodland, Christine, comps. <u>A Guide to the Papers of British Cabinet Ministers, 1900-1951</u>. Alt. subtitle: <u>1900-1964</u>. London: Royal Historical Society, 1974, 1996, 425 pp. A description of the location, contents, and accessibility of the personal papers of members of cabinets, a product of the Political Records Project; Balfour: most at British Library Add Mss 49683-49962, a total of 280 vols.

189   Herrick, Francis H. "Lord Randolph Churchill and the Popular Organization of the Conservative Party." <u>PHR</u>, 15 (June 1946): 178-91. The goal of young Conservatives led by Churchill in the late 19th century was Tory Democracy, a form of popular politics; the traditional hierarchy was sceptical; Balfour shifted over to the latter and Salisbury took office.

190   <u>A History of the Conservative Party</u> series. London: Longman, various. A 5-vol. series covering the history of the Conservative Party, 1830 to the present.

191   Hower, Edward. "A Spirited Story of the Psychic and the Colonel." <u>Smithsonian</u>, 26 (May 1995): 111-27. Re the Theosophical Society, the British Society for Psychical Research of which Balfour was President, Madame Blavatsky, and the "phenomena"; a sensational expose of fake acts.

192   Hurst, Michael. "Always Splendid and Never Isolated: Lord Salisbury and the Public Scene, 1830-1903." <u>Historian</u>, 47 (Autumn 1995):   10-14. Salisbury was uncle and mentor of Balfour; coined term "splendid isolation," describing British hegemony in the late 19th century.

193   -------. <u>Parnell and Irish Nationalism</u>. NY: Toronto UP, 1968, 117 pp. Balfour was a parliamentary leader during the regime of Parnell, the Irish leader.

194   Hutcheson, John A. <u>Leopold Maxse and the "National Review," 1893-1914: A Study in Unionist Journalism and Politics</u>. NY: Garland, 1989, 520 pp. From a revised dissertation, University of North Carolina; Maxse was a powerful journalist during the Balfour era; coined the phrase, "Balfour Must Go!"

195   <u>Index of Manuscripts in the British Library</u>. Vol. I. Cambridge: Chadwyck-Healey, 1984. A finding list of manuscripts found in the British Library; the Balfour papers are indexed, pp. 254-55, e.g., correspondence with Sir Charles Dilke, Sir Henry Campbell-Bannerman, and W.E. Gladstone.

196   Inwood, Stephen. "The Role of the Press in English Politics during the First World War." D.Phil. diss, Oxford, 1971. A dissertation on the influence of the press during the Balfour era.

197   Irving, John J. The Smoke Screen of Jutland. NY: McKay; London: Kimber, 1966, 1967, 256 pp. A critique of the battle and aftermath by a young participant, written later, pro-Jellicoe who was compared to Nelson; coverage of the German and British communiques and consequences.

198   Jackson, Sir William and Bramall, Lord. The Chiefs: The Story of the United Kingdom Chiefs of Staff. Washington: Brassey; NY: Macmillan, 1992, 1993, 530 pp. A comprehensive history of the top military organization; a chapter (pp. 25-52) on the rise and fall of CID; credited Balfour as founder.

199   Jay, Richard. Joseph Chamberlain: A Political Study. NY: Oxford UP, 1981, 393 pp. A political analysis of the career of Chamberlain who twice tried and failed to transform British politics, in the 1880s and 1900s.

200   Jeffries, Joseph M.N. The Balfour Declaration. Beruit: Institute of Palestine, 1967, 20 pp. An explanatory pamphlet.

201   Jenkins, Roy. Asquith: Portrait of a Man and an Era. London: Collins; Macmillan; NY: Chilmark, 1964, 1965, 1967, 1994, 572 pp. A revisionist biography of Asquith by a prominent Labor MP and President of the European Commission; details on the political and social life of Asquith, especially relations with Venetia Stanley.

202   -------. Gladstone. London: Macmillan, 1996, 715 pp. A new and comprehensive biography of the great Liberal statesman, mentor of Balfour during the 1870s and 1880s.

203   -------. Mr. Balfour's Poodle: Peers vs. People. Alt. subtitle: An Account of the Struggle between the House of Lords and the Government of Asquith. London: Heinemann; Collins; NY: Chilmark, 1954, 1968, 1989, 320 pp. A delightful account, frequently reprinted, of a short period of parliamentary history, the constitutional crisis leading to the Parliament Act of 1911; Lloyd George: "The House of Lords is not the watchdog of the constitution; it is Mr. Balfour's poodle" (p. 11).

204   Jones, Clyve and Jones, David L., eds. Peers, Politics and Power: The House of Lords, 1603-1911. Rio Grande, OH: Hambledon, 1986, 588 pp. A general historical survey of the House of Lords and collections of recent writing;

Balfour was directly involved in the process leading to the culmination of the book, the Parliament Act of 1911.

205 Jones, Morris R. The Education Act, 1902. London, 1903. A description of the act with supporting remarks by Balfour.

206 Jones, R.B. "Balfour's Reform of Party Organisation." BIHR, 38 (1965): 94-101. After the election defeat of 1906 there was a call to reform the party organization; some delay while the tariff reform campaign disrupted matters; then, Balfour created a professional bureaucracy preventing single issues or groups dominating and providing security for party leaders.

207 Judd, Denis O. "A.J. Balfour and the Evolution and Problems of the British Empire, 1874-1906." Ph.D. diss, London, 1966. A dissertation focusing on the role of Balfour in developments in the British Empire.

208 -------. Balfour and the British Empire: A Study in Imperial Evolution, 1874-1932. London: Macmillan; NY: St. Martin, 1968, 392 pp. Re the attitudes and policies of Balfour toward the empire culminating in the Balfour Report of 1926 and Statute of Westminster of 1931; much on the career and personality of Balfour.

209 Jullian, Philippe. Edward and the Edwardians. NY: Viking, 1967, 312 pp. Trans. from French by Peter Dawnay; a French perspective on Edward and his age, King Edward being very popular in France after the entente cordiale.

210 Kedourie, Elie. England and the Middle East: The Destruction of the Ottoman Empire, 1914-1921. London: Bowes, 1956, 1978, 1987, 248 pp. Prepared as an Oxford dissertation but director objected to a source and Kedourie refused to change it; from the Arab perspective and critical of the British; most emphasis on the making and unmaking of the Sykes-Picot agreement, dividing up the Ottoman empire.

211 -------. In the Anglo-Arab Labyrinth: The McMahon-Husayn Correspondence and Its Interpretations, 1914-1939. Cambridge: UP, 1976, 342 pp. The correspondence was the basis of the diplomacy of the Middle East and disputes over Palestine; much controversy arose over interpretations; in 1920 T.E. Lawrence wrote an expose.

212 Kekewich, Sir George W. The Education Department and After. London: Constable, 1920, 358 pp. Re the Education Act of 1902 and some of the controversy following it, especially related to objections of nonconformists; by an opponent of the Act.

213   Kelsch, Anne Airth-Kindree. "Politicians, the Press and Power: Lord Beaverbrook's Introduction to British Politics, 1910-1918." Ph.D. diss, Texas A&M, 1993, 306 pp. A dissertation about the rise of a Canadian journalist-business man into the hierarchy of the Conservative party; instrumental in ousting Balfour and succession of Bonar Law; signified a transition within the party, from the old Tories to a new business-oriented leadership.

214   Kendle, John. <u>Walter Long, Ireland, and the Union, 1905-1920</u>. Montreal: McGill-Queens UP, 1992, 246 pp. Long was a key Unionist and sometime Irish official, opposing Home Rule; when Balfour was ousted as leader in 1911, Long and Austen Chamberlain were contenders but Bonar Law succeeded.

215   Kennedy, Aubry Leo. <u>Salisbury, 1830-1903: Portrait of a Statesman</u>. London: Murray, 1953, 423 pp. A biography of the foreign policy expert and Prime Minister, uncle and mentor of Balfour.

216   Kent, Marian, ed. <u>The Great Powers and the End of the Ottoman Empire</u>. London: Allen; Cass, 1984, 1996, 247 pp. A series of essays on the Ottoman Empire and the big powers such as Britain, France, Russia, Italy, and Austria, each with vested interests; Great Britain received the Mandate for much of it.

217   Keynes, John Maynard. <u>The Economic Consequences of the Peace</u>. NY: Harcourt; NY: Penguin, 1920, 1995, 336 pp. Intro. by Robert Lekachman; the influential critique of the economic provisions of the Versailles Settlement by the famous economic theorist; Keynes, a member of the British delegation, resigned in protest.

218   Kimche, Jon. <u>The Unromantics: The Great Powers and the Balfour Declaration</u>. London: Weidenfeld, 1968, 95 pp. Preface by Lord Sieff; 50th anniversary commemoration of the declaration; sponsored by the Anglo-Israeli Association; detailed background of events leading to the Balfour Declaration.

219   Koss, Stephen E. <u>Asquith. British Political Biography</u>. London: Lane, 1976, 310 pp. A solid biography of the Prime Minister before and during the First World War.

220   -------. "British Political Biography as History." <u>Political Science Quarterly</u>, 88 (December 1973): 713-24. Political biography attained a unique place in the political culture of British society; prominent politicians wrote biographies, e.g., Rosebery, Morley, Winston Churchill, Julian Amery, and Roy Jenkins; assessed biographies of Balfour.

221   -------. <u>Fleet Street Radical: A.G. Gardiner and the "Daily News"</u>. Hamden, CT: Shoe String, 1973, 339 pp. Gardiner was another of the influential journalists active during the Balfour era.

222   -------. <u>The Rise and Fall of the Political Press in Britain</u>. 2 vols. Chapel Hill: UNCP; London: Fontana, 1981-1984, 1990, 1180 pp. Awarded the Schuyler Prize of 1986 by the American Historical Association; the standard history of the political press, at its height in the first decades of this century; informative on Edwardian political attitudes.

223   Lambert, Angela. <u>Unquiet Souls: The Indian Summer of the British Aristocracy, 1880-1918</u>. London: Macmillan, 1984, 286pp. "King Arthur or the Adored Gazelle" was featured prominently (pp. 50-71) among this elite, intellectual, country house set.

224   Lang, Marshall B. <u>The Seven Ages of an East Lothian Parish: Being the Story of Whittingehame from Earliest Times</u>. Edinburgh: Grant, 1929, 224 pp. Dedicated "To the Rt.Hon. Earl of Balfour, KG, OM and Miss Balfour"; foreword by Lady Frances Balfour; by the Very Reverand Lang, Minister of Whittingehame; linked the region to prehistoric times, cairns, stone circles, Traprain Law, Druids, St. Columba, and St. Oswald, patron saint of Whittingehame; the church was consecrated in 1245; Whittingehame Castle was linked to the murder of Darnley in the 16th century; Balfour headed the family in the 20th century.

225   Langan, Mary and Schwarz, Bill, eds. <u>Crises in the British State, 1880-1930</u>. London: Hutchinson, 1985, 288 pp. Contended that the Conservative Party only endured: Whigs, Liberals, and even Labor (in the 1980s) either fell or were falling; the tariff reform campaign, the Die Hards, the Lloyd George Coalition, and the success of Stanley Baldwin were key episodes.

226   Lawrence, Thomas Edward. <u>Revolt in Desert</u>. NY: Doran 1927, 328 pp. A memoir by Lawrence of Arabia of his experiences among the Arabs and a critique of British policies.

227   -------. The Seven Pillars of Wisdom. NY: Dell; Doubleday, 1926, 1935, 1966, 672 pp.   The better known and extensive memoir-critique by Lawrence of Arabia.

228   Lazer, Harry. "Balfourian Conservatism: A Study in Political Ideas and Political Leadership." Ph.D. diss, Columbia, 1960, 468 pp. Balfour was seen as an aristocratic dilettante whose career was marked by ineffectuality and failure; Lazer saw him as a moderate success in politics, e.g., education and temperence, but distracted by the tariff reform controversy.

229   Lebow, Richard N. "Woodrow Wilson and the Balfour Declaration." JMH, 40 (December 1968): 501-23. During the fall of 1917 Wilson first opposed the Zionist position but changed; Louis Brandeis, a prominent Zionist, influenced the change of view; others such as Leonard Stein, disagreed.

230   Lee, Alan J. The Origins of the Popular Press in England, 1855-1914. London: Croom Helm, 1976, 310 pp. An impressive study of the rising influence of journalism during the Balfour era.

231   Lee, J. The Modernization of Irish Society, 1848-1918. Dublin, 1973. A survey of the history of Irish society; included coverage of the Land League and land wars with which Balfour had to deal when he was Chief Secretary.

232   Lee, Sir Sidney. King Edward VII: A Biography. 2 vols. London: 1925-1927, 768 pp. The official biography of Edward, the symbol of the age.

233   Lees-Milne, James. The Enigmatic Edwardian: The Life of Reginald, Second Viscount Esher. London: Sidgwick, 1986, 411 pp. Biography of the "power behind the scenes"; access to private papers; exposed psychological and sexual abnormalities; made the persistent refusal of public office by Esher understandable.

234   Levene, Mark. "The Balfour Declaration: A Case of Mistaken Identity." ENGHISREV, 107 (January 1992): 54-77. Extensive and intensive study of the making of the Balfour Declaration and subsequent literature; analysis of various personalities; Balfour and Sykes, among others, were anti-Semites and Jews were seen as pro-German, wealthy, and powerful; Sykes converted to the Zionist position was decisive; at a crucial Cabinet meeting, 31 October 1917, Balfour favored support of Zionism for military, diplomatic, and political reasons.

235 -------. War, Jews and the New Europe: The Diplomacy of Lucien Wolf, 1914-1919. London: Oxford UP, 1992, 360 pp. A European, even a global, view of the Jewish Question; Wolf was a supporter of the Balfour Declaration.

236 Lowe, C.J. and Dockrill, M.L. The Mirage of Power: British Foreign Policy. 3 vols. Boston: Routledge, 1972, 816 pp. An extensive survey, including one volume of documents, British foreign policy, 1902-1922; credited Weizmann with converting Zionists from pro-German to pro-Entente position (II., p. 228).

237 Lucy, Sir Henry W. The Balfourian Parliament, 1900-1905. London: Hodder, 1906, 446 pp. From a series of published diaries of a parliamentarian; the last of the series which began with the Parliament of 1874.

238 Lydgate, John E. "Curzon, Kitchener and the Problem of Indian Army Administration, 1899-1909." Ph.D. diss, London, 1965. A dissertation about the major conflict between Viceroy Curzon and General Kitchener in India, an aspect of civil-military control; the conflict created a serious crisis for the Balfour government.

239 Lyons, Francis S. Ireland Since the Famine, 1850 to the Present. London: Weidenfeld, 1971, 852 pp. A solid, scholarly, balanced, and comprehensive survey of Ireland and its history, including the late 19th century when Balfour was Chief Secretary.

240 McDermott, William J. "British Strategic Planning and the Committee of Imperial Defence, 1871 to 1907." Ph.D. diss, Toronto, 1971. A dissertation under H.I. Nelson; the Boar War demonstrated the dismal performance of the armed forces; creation of CID meant more influence from the War Office and reorientation of strategic planning from Asia to Europe.

241 McDonald, Ian. "Postcards and Politics: Cross Currents." HISTOD, 44 (January 1994): 5-9. Early in the 20th century use of picture postcards became a media event with political subjects as especially popular; of those Joseph Chamberlain and his tariff reform campaign were lionized while Balfour was mercilessly ridiculed.

242 McEwen, J.M. "'Brass-Hats' and the British Press during the First World War." Canadian Journal of History, 18 (April 1983): 43-67. Another example of the power and influence of the press; "Brass-Hats" were high ranking officers, e.g., Kitchener, Fisher, and Jellicoe; the most influential journalists included A.G. Gardiner, C.P. Scott, J.A. Spender, and most vociferous, J.L. Garvin.

243   McFall, David.   Sculptor of Statue of Balfour.   The official parliamentary statue of Balfour, 7-ft. high in French limestone by McFall, was unveiled by Harold Macmillan in the Members' Lobby, House of Commons, 9 May 1962, located next to Asquith; an earlier model with a golf cap was rejected.

244   McIntyre, W. David. The Commonwealth of Nations: Origins and Impact, 1869-1971. Minneapolis: UMinnP, 1977, 614 pp. A survey of the making of the Commonwealth; noted the significance of the Balfour Report of 1926 as the basis of the Statute of Westminster of 1931, the constitution.

245   Mackay, Ruddock F. Balfour: Intellectual Statesman. NY: Oxford UP, 1985, 388 pp. A recent, scholarly biography; Balfour was preeminently a debater; a politician without ambition, he "inherited" offices, including that of Prime Minister; emphasis on reforms in education, domestic and foreign policies, and CID; notable diplomatic achievements included missions to the U.S.; less on personal life than in Egremont.

246   -------. Fisher of Kilverstone. NY: Oxford UP, 1973, 1974, 539 pp. An important biography of the notorious naval leader and reformer; shows the towering personality became less lovable with time; vindictive and abusive toward Beresford, Prince Louis of Battenberg, and especially Churchill; his real reforms were materiel, manning, and improved conditions and weakest on matters of strategy and war planning; stressed special relationships with journalists.

247   MacLeod, Roy M. and Andrews, E.K. "Scientific Advice in the War at Sea, 1915-1917: The Board of Invention and Research." Journal of Contemporary History, 6 (1971): 3-40. In July 1915, Balfour as First Lord created the board with Fisher as chair to screen scientific problems and determine applicability; the action was the result of failures and shortcomings, e.g., in air and in anti-submarine warfare; the scientists were given superior influence; the most enduring work was in ASW was ASDIC, soundwave based detection of submarines.

248   McTague, John J. British Policy in Palestine, 1917-1922. NY: UP of America, 1983, 286 pp.   Included much about Balfour and the Balfour Declaration; the "thrice-promised land" is the title of a chapter; much credit to Herbert Samuel and Mark Sykes.

249   Maehl, W.H. "The British General Election of 1874." Ph.D. diss,
Chicago, 1957, 109 pp. A dissertation on the election in which Balfour first
entered Parliament, for Hertford.

250   Malcolm, Sir Ian. Lord Balfour: A Memory. London: Macmillan,
1930, 136 pp. An informative memoir by the political secretary of Balfour on
the occasion Balfour's death; recollections of many events and an assessment of
the character of Balfour.

251   Mansergh, Nicholas. The Commonwealth Experience. NY: Praeger,
1969, 493 pp. A history of the Commonwealth; the making of its constitution
began during a conference of 1918, the study headed by Balfour at a later
conference in 1926, the Balfour Report, followed by the Statute of Westminster
of 1931.

252   Mansfield, Peter. The Ottoman Empire and Its Successors. The Making
of the Twentieth Century series. NY: St. Martin's, 1973, 210 pp. A general
overview of the disposition of the Ottoman Empire in an outstanding series.

253   Marder, Arthur J. From DREADNOUGHT to Scapa Flow: The Royal
Navy in the Fisher Era, 1904-1919. 5 vols. London: Oxford UP, 1961-1970,
1978, 1900 pp. The standard history of the Royal Navy, although some
revisionism has emerged; the Balfour regime at the Admiralty was covered in
vols. II and III, the latter, covering the battle of Jutland, being revised in 1978;
details on British communique authored by Balfour (III., pp. 233-43).

254   Marsh, Peter. The Discipline of Popular Government: Lord Salisbury's
Domestic Statecraft, 1881-1902. NY: Humanities, 1978, 380 pp. The latest and
best survey of the Salisbury government in which Balfour was closest to
Salisbury; Salisbury opposed popular government but adapted; rehibilitation of
Salisbury.

255   -------. Joseph Chamberlain: Entrepreneur in Politics. New Haven:
Yale UP, 1994, 742 pp.   An intensively researched new biography of
Chamberlain; unusual for a British politician to come from a business
background, then into politics where he rose rapidly, in the process causing splits
in two political parties; Chamberlain was considered for Prime Minister more
than once; seen as the first modern politician.

256   Marston, F.S. The Peace Conference of 1919: Organization and
Procedure. NY: Oxford UP; AMS, 1944, 1978, 287 pp. Foreword by C.K.
Webster; a description of the structure and operations of the peace conference;

Balfour was a member of the Council of Ten and presided over the British Empire delegation; on 22 February 1919 the Balfour Resolution was passed.

257 Martin, G.H. and Spufford, Peter, eds. The Records of the Nation: The Public Record Office, 1838-1988, the British Records Society, 1988-1988. Rochester: Boydell, 1990, 320 pp. For the British Records Society; 15 essays from a commemoration (150th and 100th anniversaries) conference, August 1988; e.g., an essay on the 30-year rule and on types of record holdings.

258 Massie, Robert K. DREADNOUGHT: Britain, Germany, and the Coming of the Great War. London: Cape; NY: Random House; Ballantine, 1991, 1992, 1028 pp. A massive tome, a popular, anecdotal approach with numerous biographical essays; DREADNOUGHT is not introduced until chapter 26 of 46 chapters; Balfour (pp. 310-24) figured as the choice of Prime Minister over Joseph Chamberlain in 1902; sources are generally out of date.

259 Matthew, H.C.G. Gladstone. 2 vols. London: Oxford UP, 1986-1995, 1434 pp. The latest and most comprehensive biography of the great Liberal prime minister and mentor of Balfour; complements the recently completed Gladstone Diaries, 14 vols.

260 Meade, Marion. Madame Blavatsky: The Woman Behind the Myth. NY: Putnam, 1980, 582 pp. A biography of the notorious leader of the Theosophical Society.

261 Medlicott, W.N. The Congress of Berlin and After: A Diplomatic History of the Near Eastern Settlement, 1878-1880. London: Methuen, 1938, 442 pp. Balfour was secretary to Salisbury at this famous European conference.

262 Mendelssohn, Peter de. The Age of Churchill. Vol. I.: Heritage and Adventure, 1874-1911. NY: Knopf; London: Thames, 1961, 661 pp. By a political journalist; intended to be a 3-vol. biography and touted to incorporate Lord Randolph and Winston "as one consecutive whole" and as "the Churchillian century" (p. 3); only this volume completed; informative on Fisher-Garvin relationship and on the 1909-1911 period.

263 The Metaphysical Society. Founded in 1869 and lasted to 1881. Balfour was one of 62 members, e.g., Morley, Ruskin, Gladstone, and Huxley; a coterie of Victorian intellectuals; abstract philosophical discussions.

264 Meter, Robert H. Van, Jr. "The Washington Conference of 1921-1922: A New Look." Pacific Historical Review, 46 (November 1977): 603-24.

Emphasis on 4 issues: naval rivalry, the Open Door policy toward China, economic concerns, and political pressures in the U.S.

265   Miliband, Marion, ed. The "Observer" of the Nineteenth Century, 1791-1901. London: Longman, 1966, 296 pp. Intro. by Asa Briggs; the Observer exerted political influence; J.L. Garvin was editor later.

266   Minney, R.J. The Edwardian Age. Boston: Little, 1965, 224 pp. Recaptured the elegance and splendor of the famous age.

267   Moncure, James A., ed. Research Guide to European Historical Biography. 4 vols. Washington: Beacham, 1992, 2270 pp. 197 mini-biographies of prominent European leaders; Balfour entry by Rasor (I., pp. 104-12).

268   Monger, George W. The End of Isolation: British Foreign Policy, 1900-1907. London: Nelson, 1963, 343 pp. This transformation in British foreign policy occurred during the Salisbury and Balfour governments; agreements with Japan, France, and Russia were prominent.

269   -------. "The End of Isolation: British Foreign Policy, 1900-1905." Ph.D. diss, Cambridge, 1961. The dissertation upon which the previous entry was based.

270   Monroe, Elizabeth. Britain's Moment in the Middle East, 1914-1956. Baltimore: Johns Hopkins UP, 1963, 1981, 254 pp. Foreword by Peter Mansfield; focused of the British Cabinet and the "Garden Suburb" of Lloyd George, especially Mark Sykes; noted the important role of oil.

271   Montagu, Edwin S. Edwin Montagu and the Balfour Declaration. London: Arab League, 1966, 24 pp. From papers of Montagu, the only Jew in the Cabinet, after the 50-year rule; Montagu opposed British Zionism and the Balfour Declaration; saw Zionism as a threat to the patriotism and loyalty of British Jews; saw the Balfour Declaration as an anti-Semitic act and an injustice to Arabs.

272   Morris, A.J. The Scaremongers: The Advocacy of War and Rearmament, 1896-1914. Boston: Routledge, 1984, 495 pp. An account of jingo, yellow, patriotic journalists before World War I, e.g., Leo Maxse, J.L. Garvin, Northcliffe, and Repington; alleged manipulation, e.g., by Fisher and Beresford; concluded that claims of conspiracy of journalists and war scares causing the war were myth; not so, the cabinet generally ignored them and made no effort to inform the public.

273   Munson, J.E.B. "The Unionist Coalition and Education, 1895-1902." HJ, 29 (September 1977): 607-45. About the making of the Education Act of 1902; credit should also be given to the Fabian Society; noted political and educational complexities.

274   Murphy, Richard. "Faction in the Conservative Party and the Home Rule Crisis, 1912-1914." History, 71 (June 1986): 222-34. Irish Home Rule was the most bitter political issue and the Conservative Party was subjected to factions related to tariff reform, the Parliament Act of 1911, and succession of leadership after Balfour; the Home Rule issue has been neglected.

275   Murray, Bruce K. The People's Budget, 1909-1910: Lloyd George and Liberal Politics. NY: Oxford UP, 1980, 352 pp. Expansion of social programs and DREADNOUGHTS were costly and Lloyd George made a deliberate decision for direct taxation, a tax on wealth, for the People's Budget of 1909; this was a break from previous financial strategy.

276   Muslih, Muhammad Y. The Origins of Palestinian Nationalism. NY: Columbia UP, 1988, 288 pp. Covered the late 19th and early 20th century; factors were the Ottoman Empire, the Young Turk period, and the Arab reaction to Zionism; led to some political organization of Palestinian nationalism.

277   National Register of Archives (Scotland). Edinburgh. Included the Whittingehame collection, Balfour's papers; access is gained through this office; also see the Scottish Record Office, Edinburgh.

278   Neher-Bernheim, Renee. La declaration Balfour, 1917: Creation d'un foyer national juif en Palestine. Paris, 1969, 472 pp. A French account of the Balfour Declaration.

279   Nevakivi, Jukka. Britain, France and the Arab Middle East, 1914-1920. London: Athlone, 1969, 298 pp. From a London dissertation, a neglected topic overshadowed by the European settlement; caused deterioration of Anglo-French relations; disputes over the disposition of Syria and Palestine and over the Sykes-Picot Agreement.

280   Newton, Scott and Porter, Dilwyn, comps. Joseph Chamberlain, 1836-1914: A Bibliography. Bibliographies and Indexes in World History # 32.

Westport: Greenwood, 1994, 157 pp. A recent extensive bibliography on all aspects about Joseph Chamberlain.

281 Nicholson, Rev. A. The Immoraltiy of Naturalism: A Sermon on the Rt. Hon. A.J. Balfour's "Foundations of Belief". Birmingham: Cornish, 1896, 12 pp. A pamphlet from a collection of sermons; Nicholson was minister of St. Albans, Leamington; praise for the work of Balfour and naturalism.

282 Nicolson, Sir Harold. Curzon: The Last Phase, 1919-1925. NY: Longman, 1939. Sir Harold wrote this partial biography of Curzon as Foreign Secretary; the theme was the practice of traditional diplomacy in the settlement of the postwar world.

283 -------. King George V: His Life and Reign. NY: Doubleday, 1953, 593 pp. A sound and solid narrative history of the reign of the king who was credited with bringing stability back to the monarchy, the king after Edward VII; informative on the crisis associated with the House of Lords.

284 -------. Peacekeeping 1919. London: Methuen; NY: University; Smith, 1933, 1944, 1964, 402 pp. A survey of the peace conference of Versailles, Balfour playing an important role.

285 Nish, Ian H. Alliance in Decline: A Study in Anglo-Japanese Relations, 1908-1923. University of London Historical Studies # 33. NY: Oxford UP; London: Athlone, 1972, 436 pp. Re a series of revisions of the original alliance, culminating in the Washington Conference; Balfour played a role in the beginning and the end of the Anglo-Japanese Alliance.

286 -------. The Anglo-Japanese Alliance: The Diplomacy of Two Island Empires, 1894-1907. University of London Historical Studies # 18. NY: Oxford UP, 1966, 420 pp. The standard survey in English by a noted expert on Anglo-Japanese relations.

287 Noamani, I.T. "The Theism of Lord Balfour." HISTOD, 17 (October 1967): 660-66. On the occasion of the 50th anniversary of the Balfour Declaration; re a remarkable British statesman, also an eminent theist and philosopher, a brilliant amateur.

288 Nowell-Smith, Simon, ed. Edwardian England, 1901-1914. NY: Oxford UP, 1964, 619 pp. A series of 15 essays by experts on various aspects of the era, e.g., on the Royal Navy and Jacky Fisher.

289   O'Brien, Phillips P. "The Cabinet, Admiralty and the Perceptions Governing the Formation of British Naval Policy, 1900-1937." Ph.D. diss, Cambridge, 1992. A dissertation under Zara Steiner; focused on policy formulation during 3 crucial periods, 1909, 1921-1922, and the interwar period; the tension between the desired fleet and economic constraints.

290   O'Callaghan, Margaret. British High Politics and a Nationalist Ireland: Criminality, Land and the Law under Forster and Balfour. Cork: UP, 1994, 223 pp. An impressive presentation and reinterpretation involving several levels: Liberal vs. Conservative, differing images and perceptions of the Irish people, high and low politics, land and nationality, and Forster and Balfour.

291   Olson, William J. Britain's Elusive Empire in the Middle East, 1900-1921: An Annotated Bibliography. NY: Garland, 1982, 422 pp. An informative introduction and 664 annotated entries; factors included India, the decline of the Ottoman Empire, and the roles of France and Russia.

292   Oppenheim, Janet. "A Mother's Role, a Daughter's Duty: Lady Blanche Balfour, Eleanor Sidgwick, and Feminist Perspectives." Journal of British Studies, 34 (April 1995): 196-232. Re the mother and sister of Balfour, the latter marrying Henry Sidgwick of Cambridge University; noted Lady Blanche had run two estates and Balfour let Whittingehame run down.

293   -------. The Other World: Spiritualism and Psychical Research in England, 1850-1914. NY: Cambridge UP, 1985, 503 pp. An extensive presentation putting each in context; Balfour was involved.

294   Parker, James G., ed. Lord Curzon, 1859-1925: A Bibliography. Bibliographies of British Statesmen series # 5. Westport: Greenwood, 1991, 136 pp. Curzon, 1859-1925, was Foreign Minister after Balfour; 594 entries.

295   Parliamentary Debates. Hansard. London: HMSO, various. Hundreds of volumes; verbatim accounts of all of the debates in the House of Commons and House of Lords; Balfour was in the House of Commons until 1922, then the House of Lords.

296   Paterson, John. Edwardians: London Life and Letters, 1900-1914. Chicago: Dee; Lancaster: Gazelle, 1996, 352 pp. A social and cultural history of the age; the Souls, sex, suffragettes, and strikes; what was needed: a sacrificial war to regenerate the nation.

297   Pearson, Karl. Reaction!: A Criticism of Mr. Balfour's Attack on
Rationalism. London: Reeves, 1895, 40 pp. A critique of an address by
Salisbury on politics and science and The Foundations of Belief by Balfour, the
one pseudo-science and the other pseudo-psychology; the latter was a better
theologian than politician; predicted Balfour will fail as a politician.

298   Peel, A.G.V. Imperial Preference, 1894-1945. Free Trade Union
Pamphlets # 2. London: Free Trade Union, 1945, 23 pp. A pamphlet
describing an aspect of the tariff reform campaign, exclusivity of imperial trade.

299   -------. The Tariff Reformers. London: Methuen, 1913, 194 pp.
About the leaders of the tariff reform movement.

300   Pearson, Lilian M. Foreign Affairs under the Third Marquess of
Salisbury. London: Athlone, 1962, 21 pp. A pamphlet about the foreign policy
activities of Salisbury, e.g., the Congress of Berlin and cooperation with the
Triple Alliance.

301   -------. "The New Course in British Foreign Policy, 1892-1902." Royal
Historical Society Transactions, 4th ser, 25 (1943): 121-38. The policy was
characterized by cooperation with the Triple Alliance but that will soon change.

302   Phillips, Gregory D. The Diehards: Aristocratic Society and Politics
in Edwardian England. Cambridge: Harvard UP, 1979, 236 pp. A study of
British aristocracy; began with the Liberal victory of 1906; Conservatives
maintained a majority in the House of Lords; obstructed social reform and the
budget; the Parliament Act of 1911 resolved the crisis but 113 of 590 Lords
voted against it, the Diehards; noted the majority were active in politics.

303   Poe, Bryce. "British Army Reforms, 1902-1914." Military Affairs, 31
(Fall 1967): 131-38. After the imbroglio of the Boer War, Balfour appointed
Royal Commissions, one headed by Lord Esher; one outcome was establishment
of CID, a significant innovation.

304   Powell, David. The Edwardian Crisis: Britain, 1901-1914. British
History in Perspective series. NY: St. Martin's; London: Macmillan, 1996, 224
pp. A recent reassessment of the Edwardian era, focusing on the series of
domestic crises.

305   Quinault, R.E. "The Fourth Party and the Conservative Opposition to
Bradlaugh, 1880-1888." ENGHISREV, 91 (April 1976): 315-40. Charles
Bradlaugh was the subject of prolonged controversy within the House of

Commons; ambitious and unscrupulous Tories created obstruction; Balfour "was, at best, only an associate member. . . ." (p. 323).

306   Ramsden, John A.   The Age of Balfour and Baldwin, 1902-1940.   A History of the Conservative Party, 1832-1975 # 3 of 5.   London: Longman, 1978, 427 pp.   One of a 5-vol. history of the Conservative Party; Ramsden has superseded Robert Blake as historian of the party; the theme was retreat and recovery, "disaster" and "drift" being the terms describing the Balfour period.

307   Rasor, Eugene L.   The Battle of Jutland: A Bibliography. Bibliographies of Battles and Leaders series # 7.   Westport: Greenwood, 1991, 190 pp.   A historiographical/bibliographical survey of the battle of 1916 with 528 annotated entries; Balfour was First Lord and wrote the communique after the battle.

308   -------.   British Naval History since 1815: A Guide to the Literature. Military History Bibliographies series # 13.   NY: Garland, 1990, 864 pp.   A historiographical survey of the Royal Navy with 3125 entries; Balfour maintained close contact and was First Lord during the period.

309   Rayleigh, Lord Robert.   Lord Balfour in His Relation to Science. Cambridge: UP, 1930, 46 pp.   A memoir by the brother-in-law of Balfour on the occasion of his death; noted the role of science and philosophy and that of the Royal Society on the life of Balfour.

310   Reinharz, Jehuda.   "The Balfour Declaration and Its Maker: A Reassessment."   JMODHIS, 64 (September 1992):   455-99.   Re Chaim Weizmann, British leader of the Zionist movement; Balfour met Weizmann several years before the Declaration; he and other government officials maintained that contact.

311   -------.   Chaim Weizmann. 2 vols.   London: Oxford UP, 1985-1993, 1124 pp.   Two of a proposed 3-vol. biography of Weizmann, most influential in the making of the Balfour Declaration and the first president of the state of Israel; on the Balfour Declaration (II., pp. 172-212).

312   -------.   "Chaim Weizmann: The Shaping of a Zionist Leader before the First World War."   Journal of Contemporary History, 18 (April 1983): 205-32. Weizmann was credited with the making of the Balfour Declaration.

313   -------.   "His Majesty's Zionist Emissary: Chaim Weizmann's Mission to Gibraltar in 1917."   Journal of Contemporary History, 27 (April 1992): 259-

77. Weizmann was instrumental in deflecting an American special diplomatic mission in 1917 concerning the Ottoman Empire.

314   Rempel, Richard A. <u>Unionists Divided: Arthur Balfour, Joseph Chamberlain and the Unionist Free Traders</u>. Newton Abbot: David; Hamden: Archon, 1972, 236 pp. Unionist Free Traders were opponents of the Tariff Reform campaign of Chamberlain; the controversy seriously disrupted the party; Balfour was replaced as party leader.

315   Rhodes James, Sir Robert. <u>Lord Randolph Churchill</u>. London: Weidenfeld, 1959, 1995, 384 pp. A political biography of the powerful Conservative leader, the most prominent member of the Fourth Party, who acted with decreasing rationality, later going insane.

316   Riddell, Lord George. "Arthur Balfour." <u>Country Life</u> (March 1930). A short article in a popular magazine by an influential journalist.

317   -------. <u>The Riddell Diaries, 1908-1923</u>. London: Athline, 1986, 448 pp. Ed. by J.M. McEwen; foreword by John Grigg; Riddell was an influential journalist and insider who was critical of Balfour and his service in the war cabinet.

318   Ridley, Jane and Percy, Clayre, eds. <u>The Letters of Arthur Balfour and Lady Elcho, 1885-1917</u>. London: Hamilton, 1992, 392 pp. A revealing set of 130 letters, correspondence between Balfour and an intimate friend from the days of the Souls; the Elcho family withdrew the letters from public access at the British Library, now released again; not love letters and much about politics and society; her letters were longer and more revealing than his.

319   Roach, John. <u>Secondary Education in England, 1870-1902: Public Activity and Private Enterprise</u>. NY: Routledge, 1991, 293 pp. Background coverage for the Education Act of 1902; focused on secondary education.

320   Robbins, Keith, ed. <u>Bibliography of Writings on British History, 1914-1989</u>. Oxford: Clarendon, 1996, 957 pp. An extensive bibliography with 27,264 entries on all aspects of British history, e.g., sections on publications about the First World War and Prime Ministers.

321   -------, ed. <u>The Blackwell Biographical Dictionary of British Political Life in the Twentieth Century</u>. Oxford: Blackwell, 1990, 463 pp. A series of minibiographies of political leaders of the 20th century; Balfour was "a crucial transition-figure" with a long ministerial career (pp. 34-37).

322 Roberts, Andrew. [A Life of Lord Salisbury]. Noted as forthcoming. Roberts is preparing an authorized biography of the Prime Minister, uncle of Balfour.

323 Rose, I.A. "The Conservative Dimension of Foreign Policy: The Conservative Party and Foreign Policy during the Lloyd George Coalition, 1918-1922." D.Phil. diss, Oxford, 1994. The European system was restructured after the First World War; members of the Conservative Party debated this matter.

324 Rose, Kenneth. The Later Cecils. London: Weidenfeld; NY: Harper, 1975, 406 pp. Cecils were ministers of the Crown 3 times in 3 centuries, 4 if Balfour, son of a female Cecil, is counted; focused on 5 sons and 2 daughters of Third Marquess; all remained Unionist Free Traders and Balfour was seen as abandoning traditional Conservatism.

325 -------. Superior Person: A Portrait of Curzon and His Circle in Late Victorian England. London: Weidenfeld, 1969, 1985, 490 pp. Balfour was an important member of Curzon's circle; both were prominent in the Souls.

326 Rose, Norman. Chaim Weizmann: A Biography. NY: Penguin, 1986, 1989, 534 pp. Many references to Balfour and the Balfour Declaration.

327 Roskill, Stephen W. Hankey: Man of Secrets. 3 vols. London: Collins, 1970-1974, 1978 pp. First access to Hankey papers; the definitive biography of an influential civil servant, secretary to CID and the War Cabinet; at the center of most important political and strategic activities for decades.

328 -------. "Lord Hankey: The Creation of the Machinery of Government: Chesney Memorial Lecture, 12 March 1975." JRUSI, 120 (September 1975): 10-18. A succinct survey of the unique position and influence of Hankey, e.g., the tank, use of convoys, and the Dardanelles campaign.

329 Rothwell, Victor H. British War Aims and Peace Diplomacy, 1914-1918. London: Oxford UP, 1971, 315 pp. Balfour was Foreign Secretary during the later stages; little coordination with the War Office.

330 Royal Historical Society British Bibliographies. London: Royal Historical Society, 1990-1997. Ed. by John Morrill, an ambitious project of the Society to compile a bibliography of 250,000 titles on British and Irish history in one computerized database on CD-ROM, estimated cost 500 pounds; the project was based in Cambridge and included books and articles.

331   Rubinstein, W.D. A History of the Jews in the English-Speaking World: Great Britain. London: Macmillan; NY: St. Martin's, 1996, 547 pp. Zionism was not important among Anglo-Jewry, then, prominent leaders caused change, especially Weizmann; the Balfour Declaration was a victory for the Zionists, despite the Jewish community rather than because of it; the fact of war was decisive, i.e., not conceivable in peacetime.

332   Russell, Alan. Liberal Landslide: The General Election of 1906. Elections and Administrations series. Newton Abbot: David; Hamden, CT: Archon, 1973, 260 pp. From an Oxford dissertation; an analysis of this crucial election, a humiliating defeat for Balfour and the Unionists; issues included fiscal, religion, education, social, Chinese labor, and the Labor Party; Balfour and Chamberlain did everything wrong.

333   Salisbury Papers. Hatfield House in Hertfordshire. Papers of the Third Marquess, Prime Minister and mentor to Balfour.

334   Sandars, J.S. Studies of Yesterday, by a Privy Councillor. London: Allan, 1928, 231 pp. Secretary to Balfour; informative; critical of Balfour for accepting Earldom.

335   Sandars Papers. Bodleian Library, Oxford. Papers of the secretary to Balfour.

336   Sanders, Ronald. The High Walls of Jerusalem: History of the Balfour Declaration and the Birth of the British Mandate for Palestine. NY: Holt, 1983, 1984, 766 pp. A fascinating account of Zionism in Britain; early contacts between Weizmann and Balfour; noted disagreements within British government; the making of the Balfour Declaration; Balfour: "one of the most complex men ever to have held the office of Prime Minister" (p. 114).

337   Scally, Robert J. The Origins of the Lloyd George Coalition: The Politics of Social-Imperialism, 1900-1918. Princeton: UP, 1975, 408 pp. An informative study; the actual coalition lasted from 1916 into the early 1920s; issues related to the origins were the tariff reform movement, the budget and the Lords, National Efficiency, and Social-Imperialism.

338   Scammell, J.M. "Spenser Wilkinson and the Defense of Britain." Military Affairs, 4 (1940): 129-42. A influential journalist-writer-academic, supporter of the concept of the Prussian General Staff; later professor at Oxford.

339   Schmitt, Bernadotte E. and Vedeler, Harold C. The World in the Crucible, 1914-1919. The Rise of Modern Europe series. NY: Harper, 1984, 573 pp. An important series; Schmitt died in 1969; the definitive survey of Europe and the war; included coverage of the Middle East and the Balfour Declaration (pp. 502-04).

340   Schults, Raymond L. Crusader in Babylon: W.T. Stead and the "Pall Mall Gazette". Lincoln: U Nebraska P, 1972, 277 pp. Stead was a founder of "the new journalism"; not really a biography or a history; the motives of Stead remain obscure.

341   Schurman, Donald M. "Imperial Defence, 1868-1887: A Study in Decisive Impulses behind the Change from 'Colonial' to 'Imperial' Defence." Ph.D. diss, Cambridge, 1955. An important dissertation about early efforts to broaden British securtiy and develop strategic doctrine; the culmination was CID.

342   Searle, G.R. Corruption in British Politics, 1895-1930. London: Oxford UP, 1987, 464 pp. Coverage of a series of scandals in the early 20th century, e.g., Marconi and honors trafficking; Balfour held 60 directorships when he became Prime Minister and he lost much money when a company collapsed.

343   -------. The Quest for National Efficiency: A Study in British Politics and British Political Thought, 1899-1914. Berkeley: UCalP, 1971, 286 pp. A subject of much interest and comment, then and now; originated after debacle of Boer War; case studies included the Education Act of 1902 and CID.

344   Selborne, Earl William. The Crisis of British Power: The Imperial and Naval Papers of the Second Earl of Selborne, 1895-1910. London: Historians, 1990, 284 pp. Ed. by D. George Boyce; Selborne was a cousin of Balfour and First Lord of the Admiralty, 1900-1905; focused on the Unionist Party; naval reforms and tariff reform movement were covered.

345   Seldon, Anthony and Ball, Stuart, eds. Conservative Century: The Conservative Party since 1900. London: Oxford, 1994, 862 pp. A series of 20 essays, use of the Conservative Party papers at the Bodleian Library, Oxford; emphasis on party structure and policies; Conservatives won 17 of 28 elections after 1880; Balfour as Prime Minister was a "detached figure" heading an "accident-prone administration" (pp. 21-22); compared to that of John Major.

346   -------, ed. How Tory Governments Fall: The Tory Party in Power since 1783. London: HarperCollins, 1996, 522 pp. The pertinent essays are by Martin Pugh and Stuart Ball (pp. 189-284); Balfour consistently failed to keep

the Conservative Party together despite successes: CID, the Education Act, and
social legislation; he was too detached and aloof; he resigned prematurely in
December 1905.

347   Self, Robert C., ed. The Austen Chamberlain Diary Letters: The
Correspondence of Sir Austen Chamberlain with His Sisters, Hilda and Ida,
1916-1937. NY: Cambridge UP, 1995, 556 pp. Chamberlain was Foreign
Minister after Balfour; many references and explanation of Balfour Note of 1922.

348   Shannon, Catherine B.   Arthur J. Balfour and Ireland, 1874-1922.
Washington: Catholic UP, 1988, 378 pp. Re the role of Balfour in the shaping
of modern Ireland; began as Chief Secretary and known as "Bloody Balfour"; the
Conservative Party philosophy toward Ireland and, later, Ulster, dominated for
40 years, Balfour representing the epitome; blamed Balfour for present tragedy
of Ireland; errors and omissions abound, e.g., Curragh Mutiny.

349   Shannon, Richard. The Age of Disraeli, 1868-1881: The Rise of Tory
Democracy. Longman History of the Conservative Party. London: Longman,
1992, 453 pp. A new general survey of the Conservative Party; Balfour entered
Parliament in 1874.

350   -------. The Age of Salisbury, 1881-1902: Unionism and Empire.
Longman History of the Conservative Party. London: Longman, 1996, 569 pp.
A new general survey of the Conservative Party; Salisbury who headed 3
governments was overshadowed by Disraeli and Gladstone; headed "Hotel Cecil";
Randolph Churchill was a threat; Balfour played a key role while Irish Secretary,
defining the government; Salisbury died before the disintegration of the Unionist
Party.

351   -------. The Crisis of Imperialism, 1865-1915. Paladin History of
England series. London: Hart-Davis, 1974, 512 pp. A textbook survey of
British history including the Balfour era.

352   Sharp, Alan. The Versailles Settlement: Peacemaking in Paris, 1919.
The Making of the Twentieth Century series. London: Macmillan; NY: St.
Martin's, 1991, 254 pp. Another in this premier series; a reassessment of the
settlement; reviewed the series of problems facing the Big 3; judicious, balanced,
clear, and concise survey.

353   Sheffy, Yigal. British Intelligence in the Palestine Campaign, 1914-
1918. Studies in Intelligence series. London: Cass, 1997, 400 pp. A recent

study using latest sources, British, German, and Ottoman; concluded that Allenby enjoyed superiority much due to intelligence advantages.

354   Shorney, D.J. "Britain and Disarmament, 1916-1931." Ph.D. diss, Durham, NC, 1981. A dissertation which included the Washington Conference in which Balfour headed the British delegation.

355   Short, Wilfrid M., ed. The Mind of Arthur James Balfour: Selections from His Non-political Writings, Speeches, and Addresses, 1879-1917, Including Special Sections on America and Germany. NY: Doran, 1918, 425 pp. Short was private secretary to Balfour; wide variety of topics addressed by Balfour, e.g., Handel, golf, education, Darwin, psychical research, and tributes to Gladstone, two monarchs, and Salisbury.

356   -------, ed. Arthur James Balfour as Philosopher and Thinker. London: Longman, 1912, 560 pp. An abridged ed. in 1913; some repetition from previous entry.

357   Sidebotham, Herbert. England and Palestine: Essays towards the Restoration of the Jewish State. London: Constable, 1918, 269 pp. A contemporaneous assessment and survey.

358   Silvester, Christopher, ed. The Literary Companion to Parliament. London: Sinclair, 1996. A recent collection of case studies not based on literature as implied but on MP perceptions of important Parliamentary events, e.g., disruption by Irish MPs and the announcement by Asquith that the king was ready to appoint up to 500 peers in 1911.

359   Smith, Jeremy. The Taming of Democracy: The Conservative Party, 1880-1924. Cardiff: U Wales P, 1997, 127 pp. The most recent of several surveys of the history of the Conservative Party.

360   Snodgrass, Catherine P., ed. The County of East Lothian: The Third Statistical Account of Scotland. Edinburgh: Oliver, 1953, 476 pp. Separate essays on subregions including the Parish of Whittingehame by Rev. Marshall Lang (pp. 406-11); the largest parish with rich arable land; murderers of Darnley came from here; 1817, James Balfour of Fife purchased Whitt estate; Balfours remained prominent, Gerald's son was the Third Earl.

361   Sokolow, Nahum. History of Zionism, 1600-1918. 2 vols. London: Longman; NY: KTAV, 1919, 1969. Preface by A.J. Balfour; Balfour described early meetings with Weizmann; about earlier generations of Jews.

362   Southgate, Donald, ed. The Conservative Leadership, 1832-1932.
London: Macmillan, 1974, 277 pp. A series of essays: re Balfour by Alfred
Gollin.

363   Startt, James D. Journalists for Empire: The Imperial Debate in the
Edwardian Stately Press, 1903-1913. Contributions in Comparative Colonial
Studies. Westport, CT: Greenwood, 1991, 282 pp. Re the golden age of
editors, e.g., Garvin, Strachey, Spender, and Northcliffe; political leaders
exploited connections, especially Balfour and Garvin.

364   Stein, Leonard J. The Balfour Declaration. NY: Simon; London:
Jewish, 1961, 1983, 695 pp. A definitive study; traced the development of the
process and relationships leading to the declaration; several factors pressured for
action: the British military campaign, the role of Germany, Russia, France, the
U.S., and even Italy; Britain showed consideration for the Jewish question but
ignored the Arab question; C.P. Scott played a decisive role in getting Weizmann
and British officials together.

365   -------. Weizmann and the Balfour Declaration. London: Rehovoth,
1964, 34 pp. The Chaim Weizmann Memorial Lecture by a noted expert.

366   -------. Weizmann and England: Presidential Address to the Jewish
Historical Society, November 11, 1964.   London: Allen, 1966, 32 pp.
Informative on early life of Weizmann and settlement in England; later, 1st
president of Israel.

367   Steiner, Zara S. Britain and the Origins of the First World War. The
Making of the Twentieth Century series. London: Macmillan; NY: St.
Martin's, 1971, 1977, 180 pp. An outstanding series including volumes on the
Big Power states and origins of the war; Steiner a noted authority on British
foreign policy; began with Boer War and realignment of policies.

368   -------. "Great Britain and the Creation of the Anglo-Japanese Alliance."
JMODHIS, 31 (March 1959): 27-36. The end of splendid isolation; at the time
the British were negotiating with the Germans and feared Russian expansion; to
reduce obligations of the Royal Navy in the Far East.

369   Sykes, Alan. "The Radical Right and the Crisis of Conservatism before
the First World War." HJ, 26 (September 1983): 61-76. A crisis of ideology
and fear of national decline created divisions in the party; issues were Home
Rule, suffragettes, and tariff reform; Balfour was hesitant and was replaced; but
the right weakened and the crisis passed.

370 -------. <u>Tariff Reform in British Politics, 1903-1913</u>. Oxford: Clarendon, 1979, 365 pp. The debate over tariff reform; Chamberlain presented as panacea for problems associated with colonialism, unemployment, social reform, and shortfalls in revenue; but issues were more complex.

371 Tarkow-Naamani, Israel. "The Abandonment of 'Splendid Isolation': A Study of British Public Opinion and Diplomacy, 1895-1902." Ph.D. diss, Indiana, 1946, 185 pp. This transformation of British foreign policy was associated with the Salisbury administration.

372 Tauber, Eliezier. <u>The Arab Movements in World War I</u>. London: Cass, 1993, 334 pp. The story from the Arab perspective; various Arab revolts against the Ottoman Empire.

373 Taylor, A.J.P. <u>Beaverbrook</u>. London: Hamilton; NY: Simon, 1972, 729 pp. By a self-proclaimed insider in the high politics; famous description of Balfour, "amateur philosopher. . . . a hermaphrodite" (p. 154), contending no one had ever seen Balfour naked; biographer Mackay refuted by recounting a case of an emergency visit from the foreign office while Balfour was taking a bath: not so.

374 -------. <u>From the Boer War to the Cold War: Essays on Twentieth-Century Europe</u>. NY: Penguin, 1995, 454 pp. A collection of 70 essays by the great historian, e.g., on Roger Casement, Winston Churchill, 3 on Joseph Chamberlain, and Balfour (pp. 55-61): "Odd Man In" was the title, "a detestable man cynical, unprincipled and frivolous"; a detailed description incorporated into a review of the Young biography.

375 -------, ed. <u>Lloyd George: Twelve Essays</u>. London: Hamilton, 1971, 393 pp. Called Lloyd George "the most dynamic figure in British politics during the first half of the 20th century" (p. v); Lloyd George had actually proposed a coalition government in 1910, the actual government coming in 1916.

376 Teed, Peter. <u>Dictionary of Twentieth-Century History, 1914-1990</u>. Oxford: UP, 1992, 528 pp. A recent historical dictionary with 2000 entries; Balfour (pp. 35-36).

377 Temperley, Harold N.V., ed. <u>A History of the Peace Conference of Paris</u>. 6 vols. London: Frowde, 1920-1924. The most authoritative and comprehensive history of the conference; Balfour played a prominent role.

378   Thompson, Edward Raymond. Pseud.: E.T. Raymond. Mr. Balfour: A Biography. Alt. title: Life of Arthur James Balfour. London: Collins; Boston: Little, 1920, 289 pp. A contemporaneous biography; Balfour was known for intellectual brilliance; he engaged in religious polemics and "mysterious excursions into metaphysics" (p. 223).

379   Thompson, Joe A and Mejia, Arthur, eds. Edwardian Conservatism: Five Studies in Adaptation. London: Helm; NY: Routledge, 1988, 256 pp. A series of surveys of aspects of conservatism.

380   -------. Biographies of Lord Robert Cecil and Lord Hugh Cecil. Proposed but incomplete, Thompson died in 1991. Influential cousins and political colleagues of Balfour.

381   Thompson, Paul R. The Edwardians: The Remaking of British Society. Bloomington: Indiana UP; London: Routledge, 1975, 1992, 382 pp. An appraisal of the era with emphasis on social change.

382   Thornton, A.P. The Imperial Idea and Its Enemies: A Study in British Power. NY: St. Martin's; London: Macmillan, 1959, 1967, 1985, 406 pp. British imperialism for and against; first written at the time of the Suez crisis of 1956; an appendix, Balfour and the imperial idea.

383   Tibawi, A.L. Anglo-Arab Relations and the Question of Palestine, 1914-1921. London: Luzac, 1977, 1978, 550 pp. A statement of the Arab perspective; reviewed history of Palestine; Zionism altered the situation, ignoring the fact that Arabs lived in Palestine; chapters on perfidious Albion and Balfour Declaration (pp. 122-239).

384   -------. "T.E. Lawrence, Faisal and Weizmann: The 1919 Attempt to Secure an Arab Balfour Declaration." Middle Eastern Forum, 45 (1969): 81-90. An article about negotiations for equality for Arabs.

385   Tomes, Jason. "A.J. Balfour and British Foreign Policy: The International Thought of a Conservative Statesman." D.Phil. diss, Oxford, 1992. Balfour was involved in British foreign policy from the Congress of Berlin of 1878 through the late 1920s; he was chief British delegate to the League of Nations and the Washington Conference; Balfour was from the conservative tradition of Burke and Coleridge.

386   -------. Balfour and Foreign Policy: The International Thought of a Conservative Statesman. Cambridge: UP, 1997, 332 pp. Developed from the previous entry; involvement of the full range of issues: the Middle East, Africa, the Far East, Zionism, the League of Nations, and Great Power relations.

387   Trollope, Anthony. The Landleaguers. Ann Arbor: U Mich P, 1981, 1992, 356 pp. Ed. by R.H. Super; Trollope's last novel, unfinished, 1883 ed., 883 pp.; re the Irish uprisings of the 1880s and Balfour's policies of reaction; presented both sides.

388   Tuchman, Barbara W. Bible and Sword: England and Palestine from the Bronze Age to Balfour. NY: Funk, London: Macmillan, 1956, 1957, 1968, 425 pp. One of the early works of this popular and Pulitzer Prize-winning historian; the British role in the creation of Israel; the Balfour Declaration was the logical product of British conscience and ambition.

389   -------. The Proud Tower: A Portrait of the World before the War, 1890-1914. NY: Macmillan, 1966, pp. 528 pp. A popular assessment, mostly anecdotal and stressing personalities, of the decades before the war in Europe.

390   Turner, John, ed. Britain and the First World War. Boston: Unwin, 1988, 165 pp. A series of 7 essays on aspects of the war, the navy, the army, strategy, economic mobilization, and the empire; Bryan Ranft on the battle of Jutland; noted German claim of victory and stunned reaction of the British.

391   -------. British Politics and the Great War: Coalition and Conflict, 1915-1918. New Haven: Yale UP, 1992, 523 pp. Re the high politics of the war within Great Britain; Lloyd George was credited with winning the war but also with destroying the Liberal Party.

392   Van Thal, Herbert, ed. The Prime Ministers. 2 vols. London: Allen, 1974-1975, 810 pp. Included essay on Balfour.

393   Verete, Mayir. "The Balfour Declaration and Its Makers." Middle Eastern Studies, 6 (January 1970): 48-76. On the occasion of the 50th anniversary of the declaration; reviewed versions, interpretations, personalities, and myths; the hero was Chaim Weizmann but he was just a tool for the British officials; concluded the role of Balfour was "small" and "if there were no Zionists, Great Britain would have invented them" (p. 48); important but neglected were Herbert Samuel and Sir Mark Sykes; should have been the "Sykes Declaration" (p. 66).

394   -------. From Palmerston to Balfour: Collected Essays of Mayir Verete. London: Cass, 1992, 247 pp. Ed. by Norman Rose; intro. by Albert Hourani; by a diplomatic historian; included the previous entry.

395   Verrier, Anthony, ed. Agents of Empire: Anglo-Zionist Intelligence Operations, 1915-1919. Washington: Brassey, 1995, 342 pp. The development of the extensive British intelligence and its accomplishments contributed decisively to the success of the Allenby campaign in the Middle East; laid the foundations for the Zionist state; included contributory Jewish agents; the fall of the Asquith government brought in backers of Zionism; Sykes was particularly important.

396   Vital, David. Zionism: Zionism Trilogy. 3 vols. Oxford: UP, 1975-1987, 1349 pp. Zionism was founded by Theodor Herzl in the late 1890s and was "saved" by Chaim Weizmann; 3rd vol. included coverage of the Balfour Declaration; Balfour changed his position because of changes in the circumstances of the war; the declaration was aimed at Europe, not the Middle East (pp. 215-17).

397   Wasserstein, Bernard. Herbert Samuel: A Political Life. London: Oxford UP, 1991, 1992, 440 pp. An outstanding political biography; Samuel was a cabinet minister and early Zionist; deserved much credit for the Balfour Declaration.

398   Webb, Beatrice. Our Partnership. London: Longman, 1948, 544 pp. Ed. by Barbara Drake and M.I. Cole; her memoirs of the late 1890s and first decade of the 20th century; discussed reform in education, the Souls, and Balfour, "a sympathetic and attractive person" (pp. 248-49).

399   Webster, Charles K. The Founder of the National Home. Chaim Weizmann Memorial Lecture. Israel: Rehovoth Archive, 1955. A published lecture by the noted diplomatic historian on Weizmann; called the Balfour Declaration "the greatest act of diplomatic statesmanship of the First World War" (p. 14).

400   Weizmann, Chaim. Trial and Error: The Autobiography of Chaim Weizmann. London: Hamilton; NY: Schocken, 1949, 1966, 608 pp. The important memoir of Weizmann, most consistently involved in Zionism and the creation of Isreal.

401   -------.   Papers of Chaim Weizmann. Housed at the Weizmann Archives, Rehovoth, Israel. An important primary source on the Balfour Declaration.

402   Wells, H.G.   An Experiment in Autobiography: Discovery and Conclusions of a Very Ordinary Brain. 2 vols. London: Gollancz; NY: Macmillan, 1934, 1984, 718 pp. The memoir of the famous writer; Balfour, Joseph Chamberlain, and the Souls were included.

403   -------. Men Like Gods. London: Heron, 1969, 328 pp. A political novel, the character Cecil Burleigh was based on Balfour.

404   -------. The New Machiavelli. London: Lane, 1911, 528 pp. A political novel, the character Evesham was based on Balfour.

405   Weston, Corinne Comstock. The House of Lords and Ideological Politics: Lord Salisbury's Referendal Theory and the Conservative Party, 1846-1922. Memoirs of the American Philosophical Society # 215. Philadelphia: APS, 1995, 251 pp. In political competition with Gladstone, Salisbury formulated the referendal theory: the House of Lords was obliged to refer crucial questions, not to the other house, but to the people; thus, the veto of the House of Lords was to be perpetuated; the Parliament Act of 1911 countered the theory.

406   Westrate, Bruce. The Arab Bureau: British Policy in the Middle East, 1916-1920. University Park: Penn State UP, 1992, 256 pp. In 1916 the Arab Bureau was established in Cairo to guide British policy; included intelligence officers such as T.E. Lawrence; disputes with the India Office; the Balfour Declaration undermined the Arab Bureau; concluded that Britain would have done well to follow the recommendations of the Arab Bureau.

407   Wheare, K.C. The Constitutional Structure of the Commonwealth. Oxford: Clarendon, 1960, 215 pp. Credit to the Balfour Report from the Imperial Conference of 1926.

408   -------. The Statute of Westminister and Dominion Status. Oxford: UP, 1938, 1942, 1947, 1949, 1953, 371 pp. The importance of this statute, the modern constitution of the British Commonwealth of Nations, was overemphasized in the early 1930s; later the Balfour Report of 1926 was reassessed and its importance was stressed.

409   White, John A. Transition to Global Rivalry: Alliance Diplomacy and the Quadruple Entente, 1895-1907. Cambridge: UP, 1995, 368 pp. The Quadruple Entente, Great Britain, France, Russia, and Japan, was the product of diplomatic restructuring which sets up the Allied side for the First World War; this extended the great-power conflict to Asia; Britain demonstrated the most initiative; Balfour was involved and, at this time, Russia was feared more than Germany.

410   Whyte, Frederic. The Life of W.T. Stead. 2 vols. NY: Houghton; Garland, 1925, 1971, 733 pp. Stead continued to be one of the most influential political journalists until his death on the TITANIC in 1912.

411   Wiener, Joel H., ed. Papers for the Millions: The New Journalism in Britain, 1850s to 1914. Contributions to the Study of Mass Media # 13. Westport: Greenwood, 1988, 347 pp. A series of essays by leading scholars recounting individual cases of influential journalists and prominent officials: e.g., the former were W.T. Stead and J.A. Spender, and the latter were Fisher and Lord Esher.

412   Williams, Rhodri H. "Arthur James Balfour, Sir John Fisher and the Politics of Naval Reform, 1904-1910." Historical Research, 60 (February 1987): 80-99. The Julian Corbett Prize Essay; the Royal Navy was the object of intense interest, 1889-1914, and Fisher, above all, was drawn into political action, establishing close relations with Balfour, as Prime Minister, and after; Balfour's support, even in opposition, meant Fisher was able to hold office and continue reforms despite governmental and internal naval opposition.

413   -------. Defending the Empire: The Conservative Party and British Defence Policy, 1899-1915. New Haven: Yale UP, 1991, 306 pp. A continuation of the developments in the previous entry, again with Balfour exerting decisive influence; the key was bipartisan cooperation on military and naval matters, led by Haldane and Fisher, respectively; his leadership on CID and for the Unionist Party, in and out of office was decisive; one objective was to counter Liberal radicals such as Lloyd George; saw Balfour as a statesman and patriot; Williams has been criticized for neglect of finance and technological factors.

414   -------. "The Politics of National Defence: Arthur James Balfour and the Navy, 1904-1911." Ph.D. diss, Oxford, 1986. The dissertation upon which the two previous entries are based.

415   Williams, Robin H., ed. Salisbury-Balfour Correspondence: Letters Exchanged between the Third Marquess of Salisbury and His Nephew Arthur James Balfour, 1869-1892. Cambridge: Hertfordshire, 1988, 483 pp. Intro. by Hugh Cecil; Balfour's "political apprenticeship" was under Salisbury; from 10 vols. of correspondence; a sequel, 1893-1903, is promised.

416   Williamson, Philip. The Modernisation of Conservative Politics: The Diaries and Letters of William Bridgeman, 1904-1935. London: Historians, 1988, 280 pp. Enlightening on adjustments made by the Conservative Party during a time of political transformation, e.g., issues like Ireland, the Church, education, and Empire; cautious leadership of Balfour gave way to "new style" of Bonar Law; Bridgeman was MP and cabinet minister.

417   Williamson, Samuel R. The Politics of Grand Strategy: Britain and France Prepare for War, 1904-1914. Cambridge: Harvard UP, 1969, 1990, 428 pp. The making of the entente cordiale and the future basis of the Allies in the war.

418   Wilson, Keith M. "The Making and Putative Implementation of a British Foreign Policy of Gesture, December 1905 to August 1914: The Anglo-French Entente Revisited." Canadian Journal of History, 31 (August 1996): 227-55. The development of Anglo-French relations; influential were the Liberal Imperialists plus Esher and Balfour.

419   -------. The Policy of the Entente: Essays on the Determinants of British Foreign Policy, 1904-1914. Cambridge: UP, 1985, 224 pp. The question of British obligations related to the Entente and associated secret military talks has been interpreted differently; contended it was domestic political factors, i.e., the Conservative Party letter to the Liberals that it would support intervention to aid France in August 1914, and foreign factors, i.e., the traditional threat of Russia, which prevailed.

420   -------. A Study in the History and Politics of the "Morning Post," 1905-1926. Studies in British History. NY: Mellen, 1990, 294 pp. The political, diplomatic, and military influence of the paper; Spencer Wilkinson was editor.

421   Witherell, Larry L. "Rebel on the Right: Henry Page Croft and the Politics of Edwardian Britain, 1903-1914." Ph.D. diss, Minnesota, 1992, 647 pp. A dissertation about Croft, a right-wing Conservative, free-trader, and anti-Balfourite.

422   Woodward, David R. Trial by Friendship: Anglo-American Relations, 1917-1918. Lexington: U Kentucky P, 1993, 286 pp. A balanced perspective of Anglo-American relations at the end of the war; factors were Allied Intervention in Russia and the Balfour Mission; Balfour and Wilson were similar: intellectual, dignified, and tactful.

423   Young, Kenneth. Arthur James Balfour: The Happy Life of the Politician, Prime Minister, Statesman, and Philosopher, 1848-1930. London: Bell, 1963, 542 pp. Focused on the personal, political, and intellectual life of Balfour; credited Balfour with outstanding service in Ireland and with saving and perpetuating the Salisbury government; with creating CID, and his maintaining his participation thereon, exerted decisive influence in the decision for war in August 1914; the offer to bury Balfour in Westminster Abbey was declined and he was buried at Whittingehame; disclosures in this biography about an "affair" with Lady Elcho so upset the Elcho family that they withdrew the correspondence, returning it to Stanway House.

424   Zebel, Sydney H. Balfour: A Political Biography. The Conference of British Studies Biographies series. London: Cambridge UP, 1973, 312 pp. Claimed to be the only biography by a professional historian; a political biography with little on the personal life of Balfour; "the last of the Peelites," Balfour had a long political career, longer than anyone else in modern times, 1974-1929; some limitations to conform to the biographical series.

425 Zionist Archives, Jerusalem. An extensive collection of Zionist materials; primary sources on the background and organization of Zionism in Europe and Britain.

Author Index

NOTE: Regular type numbers indicate page numbers; italicized numbers indicate bibliographical entries.

Subject Index

About the Author

EUGENE L. RASOR has retired as Professor of History at Emory and Henry College in Virginia, after teaching there for over 30 years. His published work has concentrated on historiographical and bibliographical surveys on British naval history and the Pacific War. His most recent bibliographies are *The China-Burma-India Campaign, 1931–1945: Historiography and Annotated Bibliography* (Greenwood, 1998) and *Earl Mountbatten of Burma, 1900–1979: Historiography and Annotated Bibliography* (Greenwood, 1998).